We come togeth[...]   ne
Whose light n[...]

..   eye ne[...]

..   mind ..   gives up,

..   heart ..   grows cold.

And whose hand never

        stops reaching out.

MORE PRAYERS FOR TODAY'S CHURCH

More PRAYERS
for Today's Church

Edited by

DICK WILLIAMS

KINGSWAY PUBLICATIONS
EASTBOURNE

ISBN 0 86065 301 3

Biblical quotations are from the New International Version,
© New York International Bible Society 1978.

*Published by
Kingsway Publications in association with the Church
Pastoral Aid Society, an Anglican, evangelical society committed
to helping local churches in mission and growth.
CPAS, Athena Drive, Tachbrook Park,
Warwick CV34 8NG.*

Printed in Great Britain for
KINGSWAY PUBLICATIONS LTD
1 St. Anne's Road, Eastbourne, E. Sussex BN21 3UN by
Richard Clay Ltd, Bungay, Suffolk.
Typeset by Nuprint Services Ltd, Harpenden, Herts.

Contents

Foreword   7
Acknowledgements   8
Introduction   9

PART 1

Prayers for the Christian Year   11

9th Sunday before Christmas: the creation   11
8th Sunday before Christmas: the fall   12
7th Sunday before Christmas: the election of God's people   13
6th Sunday before Christmas: the promise of redemption   13
5th Sunday before Christmas: the remnant of Israel   14
1st Sunday in Advent: the Advent hope   15
2nd Sunday in Advent: the word of God   16
3rd Sunday in Advent: the forerunner   20
4th Sunday in Advent: the Annunciation   22
Christmas   23
Sundays after Christmas   26
Epiphany   27
Sundays after Epiphany   28
9th, 8th, 7th Sundays before Easter   30
Ash Wednesday and Lent   31
Sundays in Lent   33
Mothering Sunday   37
Palm Sunday   40
Holy Week   42
Good Friday   45
Easter   48
Sundays after Easter   53

Ascension Day   55
Pentecost   57
Trinity Sunday   60
Sundays after Pentecost and Trinity   61
Harvest   69
One World Week   74
Remembrance Sunday   77
All Saints   83
New Year   84

PART 2

Prayers for the World and the Church

The Queen, rulers and governors   87
The nation   88
The church   90
Unity   96
The church's mission   102
The sick and suffering   112
Healing ministries   118
The underprivileged   123
Society and its problems   126
Deprived young people   134
Travel and travellers   139
Science and scientists   140
Art and artists   141
Music and musicians   143
Thinkers and writers   145
Marriage and family life   146
Broken homes and families   150
Schools and colleges   153
Family, friends and home   159
Family prayers   162
Family services and Children's Services   165
Personal devotion   173
Arrow prayers   178
Prayers for healing   180

Index of writers   184

Index of topics   186

Foreword

The first edition of *Prayers for Today's Church* was like a breath of fresh air. Its use of relevant language and its variety of form in its prayers meant that it was readily and effectively used in hundreds of churches.

Even fresh things need refreshing, and now we have this new edition with so many more prayers than before on a very wide variety of themes. It will be even more welcome and usable than its predecessor.

Books of prayers are not just for use in church services (though this one will be constantly in use in worship). They act as a mind-widener for our own prayers, showing us how to pray for many matters that do not readily come on our own limited agenda. For those who find praying difficult, whether praying silently alone or with others aloud, a book like this in the language of today, freed from Elizabethan tongue-traps, is a wonderful aid. Some will take prayers and use them in a prayer gathering—a splendid way to break the ice in praying aloud; others will find prayers to use privately. Then there are those times when we go spiritually dry and we need the help of other people's prayers: such a book as this will come quickly off the shelf.

Today's Christians—members of today's church—need to pray and, like their predecessors of earlier generations, will pray in the language of their own day for the needs of the world and the church of their own day.

This book is a most welcome aid to such praying.

Michael Baughen
Bishop of Chester

Acknowledgements

The following prayers are copyright and are reproduced by permission:

by Canon Norman Autton: numbers 400–404, 417–419 and 420 are from his book *Visiting the Sick*, published by Mowbrays; numbers 415 and 416, adapted by permission from 'thou' to 'you' form, are from his book *Watch With the Sick*, published by SPCK.

by Randle Manwaring: numbers 619 and 620 are from his book *In a Time of Unbelief*, published by Henry E. Walter Ltd.

by Canon J. W. Poole: number 274 is copyright of the Provost and Chapter of Coventry Cathedral and was included in the first edition of this book.

by the Rev. John Richards: numbers 655 and 657; numbers 197, 647–654, 656, 658 are from his publication *24 Healing Prayers*.

The prayers from the Rev. M. H. Botting's collection first appeared in *Family Worship* published by CPAS, and also appeared in this book's first edition.

The prayers by Susan Williams first appeared in *Lord of Our World* published by Falcon, with the exception of prayers 102–104, and 114–121 which appeared in the first edition of this book.

Introduction

Much has happened since the first version of *Prayers For Today's Church* appeared in 1972. In this second volume I have tried to take account of this.

In the Church of England there has been the introduction of the Alternative Services Book 1980, with its revised calendar beginning on the 9th Sunday before Christmas. So the first section of the book is based upon that calendar employing the ASB's Sunday themes. In this section I am grateful to my wife for permission to use collects originally published in her book *Lord of Our World*.

The second section of the book contains intercessions relating to a wide range of concerns. While the number of contributors is much the same—sixty-eight in this edition, fifty-eight in the previous one—the range of topics is wider. It has been good to be able to include the prayer offered in Canterbury Cathedral by Pope John Paul and the prayers specially composed for the Falklands Service in St Paul's Cathedral. In addition to topics for prayer presented by the daily news media, other themes emerged from a close study of the agendas of six groups of sessions of the Church of England's General Synod. The contents also reflect something of the fresh experience and understanding of the Holy Spirit enjoyed by so many Christians in recent years.

It is in the nature of a revision that a good deal of old material must give place to new. While much of the original is retained, even more has been replaced and some of what has been kept has been shortened. The overall emphasis is upon shorter prayers. But the general character remains the same.

While this collection has many prayers which I judge to be well composed and finely phrased, there is also a homespun flavour about some which seems to me to be important. The first edition was firmly based upon the many prayers contributed in response to an appeal in the church press. Many of these were offered with great diffidence and clearly many of them had gone straight from heart to paper. The editorial problem was to find a form which did not destroy the life. This new version also contains a number of prayers like this. Their presence will, I hope, help the book retain the sense of a great family at prayer.

Writing in his introduction to the American edition of this book's first version, Alvin N. Rogness said, 'These are bracing prayers. They do not give up on people or the world . . . . Offered by today's rank and file seekers, they echo universal longings voiced by saints long ago.'

My hope is that something similar may be felt about the present book.

DICK WILLIAMS

PART 1

Prayers for the Christian Year

9th Sunday before Christmas
THE CREATION

1   Creator God, you made all things from nothing, and sustain all creation by your will alone; help us to be more aware of your power, and more willing to walk in your ways, through Jesus Christ our Lord.   Amen.

2   Father God, you made all that is, and ourselves to be part of it: help us to see creation through your eyes and help us to reflect your glory by loving one another, through Jesus Christ our Lord.   Amen.

3   God of creation, we thank you for balancing the numberless parts of your mighty universe in one divine harmony: help us to explore each part of creation in awareness of the whole and teach us how to inhabit the world and dwell in the universe, for the good of mankind and the fulfilment of your purposes, through Jesus Christ our Lord.   Amen.

4   O God, by your Word the worlds were made: help us to know that we are your creation, not self-made but God-made, not authors of truth but children of truth. Help us to listen to the universe, to listen to one another, to listen to our own being and make us ready to listen to you as you speak to us in Jesus Christ our Lord.   Amen.

5   O God of miracles, we thank you for our growing awareness of the powers of creation and our perception of its laws. Help

us to understand that nature is subject to you, not you to it; give us humility and faith so that as we see your miracles we may perceive how you are pursuing the larger law of your own will, leading creation itself to know and serve its master, through Jesus Christ our Lord.   Amen.

6   Lord and Father, make us new people, ready to worship you in spirit and in truth, with those who live by faith in the modern world, and those who died in faith before we were born, that together we may worship you in joy forever.   Amen.

7   Lord, you made the world and put it into our hands, give us a greater care for your gift, that the resources of your earth may be used for the needs of your family and all may have enough.   Amen.

8th Sunday before Christmas
THE FALL

8   O God, you made us in your own image, but we have sinned: we thank you for your love and power in granting us new birth in Christ, that in him we may find our true self and reflect your glory, now and forever.   Amen.

9   Father God, when our sins are stronger than our faith and we hide from your light, have mercy. Give us again such trust in your love and goodness that we return to our Lord, the light of the world, who exposes in order to heal and not to condemn.   Amen.

10   We praise you, Lord, for making all things well: the world, the flesh and the spirit of man itself. We grieve for the sin to which we and all mankind have turned: the pride of heart, the abuse of bodies, the corruption of society. Come to us now, O Lord, and by the power of the cross save us from the world, the flesh and the devil, through Jesus Christ our Lord.   Amen.

11   Lord, save us from fear; fear of the inner depths of the mind.

Show us the matching depth of your forgiveness and fill us
with the love which reaches every corner of the
universe.   Amen.

7th Sunday before Christmas
THE ELECTION OF GOD'S PEOPLE

12 God of Abraham, Isaac and Jacob, we thank you for your
power to make new beginnings in the life of mankind: for
calling to birth a new nation through the faith of Abraham,
the birth of Isaac and the conversion of Jacob; for revealing
your saving power and purposes in the history of your people
Israel and for taking flesh in Christ, that all who believe may
find true brotherhood in him. Give us sure confidence in the
plan which spans the ages and may we share more fully in the
power of your purposes and rejoice at all your new beginnings
in the hearts of men, through Jesus Christ our Lord.   Amen.

13 Lord of time, Lord from before our birth to beyond our death,
help us to know you in each moment. You have chosen us;
help us to keep your word, so that we may live now in the free
and greater life of God.   Amen.

14 Lord Jesus, you were rejected by the religious men of your
time. Help us in our own day to see you in unexpected people
and in unexpected places; to acknowledge your power in our
lives and in the lives of others.   Amen.

6th Sunday before Christmas
THE PROMISE OF REDEMPTION

15 When your children, O Lord, have no freedom and are
oppressed by tyranny, grant to them leaders like Moses: men
who speak with you face to face; men who communicate with
the rulers of the land. And by your outstretched hand and
holy arm, O Lord, lead your people into liberty by ways
which you shall choose, through Jesus Christ our
Lord.   Amen.

16   All-loving God, whose son died to free us from the grip of
      evil keep us alive and free in his kingdom, dead to self and
      abundantly alive to our Lord and King, who rules for
      ever.   Amen.

17   Lord Jesus, when the solar system ends you will shine
      brighter than the sun; help us now to make the light of your
      presence known in all the world, for the sake of your
      love.   Amen.

18   Awaken us and all your people, Lord, to the danger of being
      enslaved again by sin. Save your church from worshipping
      itself; save us from closing our heart to the needs of the world
      and its pain; save us from failing to love one another in spirit
      and in truth. By the death and by the resurrection of Jesus,
      lead us, O Lord, out of this bondage into the glorious liberty
      of the children of God, for his name's sake.   Amen.

5th Sunday before Christmas
THE REMNANT OF ISRAEL

19   Lord, when we feel that we are not very many and not very
      strong, open our eyes; show us a vision of your coming, so
      that we live and work today with buoyant hope, ready at all
      times for our King and Judge.   Amen.

20   Lord save your people. Save us from putting our trust in new
      technology alone, but give us love and faithfulness to heal the
      sick and feed the hungry, till your Son returns to judge the
      world.   Amen.

21   We thank you, faithful Father, that when governments and
      nations rebel against you and persecute those who worship
      you in spirit and in truth, you do not leave yourself without a
      witness. We thank you for all those who risk the wrath of
      man for faith in Christ. We praise you for their courage and
      their grace; and we ask you to comfort and defend them.
      Grant, O Lord, that they may know themselves to be a much

loved part of that great host which no man can number which worships you in life eternal, through Jesus Christ our Lord. Amen.

22 We remember, Lord, the small beginnings of the Christian church. Help us to have a special care for minority groups in our land and in our neighbourhood. Help us to affirm in them that which is good. Help us to share with them the blessings we enjoy. And may we all be led by you into a fuller understanding of the family of man under the fatherhood of God, through the saving grace of Jesus Christ our Lord. Amen.

1st Sunday in Advent
THE ADVENT HOPE

23 Jesus, risen Lord, who taught us that all mankind will one day see you as you are, and every man be seen for what he is, help us and all men everywhere to give to you the lordship of our life; that in our heart and home, at work and play, your kingdom, soon to come in power, may dawn in grace and mercy; for the glory of your name. Amen.

24 Jesus, Son of God, help us to measure the purpose of our life against the purpose of your love and to repent. Then in mercy give your healing to our hearts that when we stand before you at the last we may be one with you to the glory of God the Father; for your tender mercy's sake. Amen.

25 Lord, you will come again as surely as summer follows spring; keep us steady when the world reels about us and make us ready for the coming of your kingdom with great power and glory. Amen.

26 Lord God, your Son will come again at the end of time, but now he lives and suffers in today's people. Send us in love to those who need our time and our care, our comfort and our possessions, that we all may grow to be fully human, fully like our Lord. Amen.

27   O God, you have given us the sure promise that Jesus will
     return to judge the earth. Make us ready, we pray, for his
     royal coming, that we may consider daily what sort of people
     we ought to be and be found faithful servants, bold in our
     witness, waiting and working for our Master's return,
     whether he come at midnight or at dawn, or in the day time:
     for his name's sake.   Amen.

28   Lord Jesus, we thank you for your promise to return to this
     world, not as a baby but as a triumphant King. Keep us
     watchful against temptation and joyous in your service, for
     your name's sake.   Amen.

29   Awaken us, O Lord, that we may not stand outside your
     kingdom, but enter in with thankful hearts. To you we owe
     our new names as sons and daughters of God: help us to think
     of ourselves as those adopted by you, that we may speak with
     a living message and a sure hope; that we may live as those
     with the kingdom of heaven here in our own hearts; through
     him who is the King, Jesus Christ our Lord.   Amen.

2nd Sunday in Advent
THE WORD OF GOD

30   Grant, O Lord, that in the written word and through the
     spoken word, we may behold the living Word, our Saviour
     Jesus Christ.   Amen.

31   Father God, your promises buried in the dust of time came
     gloriously alive in Christ; keep us faithful to you for all time,
     that in your kingdom we may join the great family which
     praises you with a single voice.   Amen.

32   Lord God, your Son confounded the Scripture experts of his
     day, confound the darkness in our minds and send us light,
     that in reading your word we may see our Lord and seeing
     may believe.   Amen.

33 Father, we thank you for the Bible because rich and poor,
wise and simple, old and young, sad and happy, can find in it
the answer to their needs. We pray that your servants may
continue to translate it into the languages of all people so that
all may know that you have come to us in Christ Jesus; for his
name's sake.   Amen.

34 Heavenly Father, you have shown through the Bible the
wonder of your love for us in Christ Jesus. Help us to
understand your word with our minds and apply it in our
lives, for his name's sake.   Amen.

35 Thank you, Lord, for the Bible: for its ability to give to us
each day new vision and new power; for its capacity to reach
to the roots of inner life and to refresh them; for its power to
enter mind and spirit and fashion them anew, to beget new
life and to sustain it, we give you thanks and praise, through
Jesus Christ our Lord.   Amen.

36 O God of love and thought and speech, we thank you for
making man in your own image that he too may love and
think and speak, and in his humanity learn to hear your voice
and to reply. Help us so to know your word that we may
understand it and so to love it that we may obey it and so to
obey it that we may help it to be heard, loved and obeyed
throughout creation, for the sake of Jesus Christ our
Lord.   Amen.

37 O God, your word brings life. Bless those who cannot hear
that word and are denied its life. Move the hearts of Christian
people everywhere to right this wrong by setting forward the
work of translating and publishing the Holy Scriptures and
preaching their good news. Call to this enterprise those best
equipped to do it. Call us all to support it. And grant that by
the labours of everyone and the blessing of your Spirit, your
word may come with great clarity and great power into the
world for its salvation, through Jesus Christ our
Lord.   Amen.

38 Help those scholars, Lord, whose task it is to learn more about the Bible and its truth. Help them to know what each part meant to its writer; help them to understand the mind of its first readers; grant them thereby a surer knowledge of the whole and give to them the mind of Christ to recognize eternal truths and see their meaning for today. So may we and all your church, O Lord, be grasped afresh by the power of your living word, through Jesus Christ our Lord.   Amen.

39 Loving Lord, we remember how you gathered your disciples together and taught them. As they met then we meet now, wanting you to teach us too. Like your disciples may we know you truly. Like your disciples may we see your power. Like your disciples may we find your kingdom and follow you, now and forever.   Amen.

40 Holy Spirit of God, thank you for causing the gospels to be written. Kindle our imagination as we picture each scene. Stir our hearts as we listen to Christ's teaching. Increase our love and obedience as we learn more of the living Lord, for his name's sake.   Amen.

An Act of Praise for the Bible

41 Let us give thanks to God.

> *Praise the Lord, O my soul,*
> *and all that is within me praise his holy name.*
> *Praise the Lord, O my soul,*
> *and forget not all his benefits.*

Let God be thanked that he has given us his message written in the Law and the Prophets, in the wisdom of the Proverbs and the poetry of the Psalms, above all in the gospel of our Lord Jesus Christ, the Word made flesh.
Thanks be to God.
Let God be thanked for the Bible in English; for those who long ago gave us early translations; for those who down the years improved them, enabling the Scriptures to penetrate deeply into our national language and life.
Thanks be to God.

18

Let God be thanked that in our ever-changing language the work of creating modern translations continues. Thank him for all that the Bible means to so many in the churches and the homes of the English-speaking world.

Thanks be to God.

Let God be thanked for those who translate, publish and distribute in other languages so that all men may come to the knowledge of the gospel.

Thanks be to God.

The Power of the Printed Word: A Meditation and Prayer

42   Let us in God's presence reflect upon the power of the printed word.

The printed word can give new thoughts and ideas to millions of readers; it can survive to speak across the centuries; it can reach those who are cut off from the influence of the spoken word; it can speak intimately to people in their own homes; it can be left behind to continue its message when the spoken word is silenced.

But the printed word can be either poison or food: it can propagate lies, suspicion, and hatred—or truth, trust and friendship.

So we pray for those who are now learning to read, and that their new skills may become for them a means of knowing and loving our Lord Jesus Christ.

Lord, in your mercy, hear our prayer.

We pray also for those who teach the illiterate to read and we remember before God writers and translators, journalists and artists, printers, publishers and booksellers, that they make wise and responsible use of this power of moulding the minds of men.

Lord, in your mercy, hear our prayer.

With thanksgiving to God for what we have been able to do in the past, let us offer to him ourselves, our gifts, our possessions, to proclaim the good news of the Christian gospel through the printed word.

Lord in your mercy, hear our prayer.

3rd Sunday in Advent
THE FORERUNNER

43 Thank you, Father, for every messenger of yours who stands
unbowed in the godless spirit of our age. Thank you for those
who stand up for justice and truth before their own rights and
freedom. May their example inspire us to the same
faithfulness to Jesus Christ our Lord.   Amen.

44 O Jesus, true God and true man, bless those whom you call to
the work of the Christian ministry.
      Help them to hear your call: help them to obey it.
      Provide them abundantly with the necessities of life; save
them from love of luxury.
      Make them ambitious to do your will; save them from
worldly ambitions.
      Give them the powers of a united mind; save them from a
divided heart.
      Sustain them in their desire to give to you the whole of
their life; help them to measure their gift against the glory of
your love and the depth of eternity.
      Deepen and enlarge their knowledge of their calling; save
them from cynicism, weariness and despair.
      Help them so to possess the riches of the world to come,
that they may attain to true humanity in this.
      And inspire them so to speak your word that all mankind
might receive it, believe it, and obey it; through Jesus Christ
our Lord.   Amen.

45 We thank you, God, for making man in such a way that what
he is can respond to what you are. Bless all those whose
response to your call takes the form of service in the sacred
ministry; make perfect their desire to be your servants;
increase their understanding of man's need and your great
love. So may they find power, peace and gladness and share
the same with those whom they shall serve; through Jesus
Christ our Lord.   Amen.

46 God of the impossible, who sent John the Baptist to shout in a desert and people came to hear; send us into the desert areas of modern life with the boldness of John and the message of the coming of your Son.   Amen.

47 Lord, give us grace to know that our knowledge of you is partial and give us the mind of John the Baptist, who fully obeyed your command where he did not fully understand.   Amen.

For Bishops

48 We pray, Lord, for the bishops of the church. Grant to them a growing vision of your glory, a clear understanding of the world and a deepening love for their flock. Make them loving, strong and wise. Deliver them from loneliness and overwork. Grant them true friends, loving fellowship, sufficient rest and the blessing of a happy home. In the power of the resurrection renew in them their first love of their Lord and make them pure in heart that they may see you, O God, for the glory of your name.   Amen.

49 Great shepherd of the flock, inspire with your kindly care those whom you call to care for the ministers and pastors of your people. Help them to love each one in the spirit of the Master. Help them to discern the needs and powers of each. Help them to know when to speak and when to be silent; what to do and when to do it. And grant that those within their care may know themselves to be secure within the love of Christ and of his church, for the glory of his name.   Amen.

Retired Clergy

50 Lord Jesus Christ, on Calvary you offered your finished work to the Father: look upon all clergy who have retired, or who for other reasons have offered back their ministries to you. Grant them your peace that their faith may be strengthened and their love of you increased until they come at last unto your everlasting kingdom, O Saviour, who with the Father

and the Holy Spirit lives and reigns for ever and
ever.   Amen.

Theological Colleges

51   Father of Jesus, Teacher of men, bless the work of all
theological colleges. Guide those who govern them; instruct
those who teach in them; make disciples of those who study
in them; and grant to all a rich and happy community life in
which diversity of mind, through unity of spirit, may glorify
Christ, for the worth of his name and the spread of his
kingdom.   Amen.

4th Sunday in Advent
THE ANNUNCIATION

52   All-demanding loving Father, you call us to work beyond our
human powers; send us your command and the gift of your
Holy Spirit, that our lives may bring in your promises and
declare the greatness of our Lord.   Amen.

53   God of the impossible, whose angel spoke of Isaac's birth and
Sarah laughed, give to us the mind of Mary, who heard a
greater promise and believed, that as your spirit speaks in our
hearts, so it may be in our lives, through Jesus Christ our
Lord, obedient to death and King for ever.   Amen.

54   Thank you, Lord, that in the fullness of time you sent your
Son to be our Saviour. We believe that in the fullness of time
he will be coming to be our King. Set alight the spark of hope
and confidence in our hearts, that we may live as those who
have a sure and certain goal in Jesus Christ our
Lord.   Amen.

55   Creator Spirit, source of life, fountain head of flesh and blood,
we rejoice to know that in the womb of a strong and humble
girl you were the source of that life known to history and to us
as Jesus.   Amen.

56 Like the dying thief, O Lord, we leave our most important
decisions almost too late. Our life lies open to you like a
book. Forgive the sins we have not thought about or
confessed. We have no merit of our own, but you have paid
our debts. We call upon your love. Amen.

CHRISTMAS

57 O God our Father, as we remember the birth of your Son,
Jesus Christ, we welcome him with gladness as Saviour and
pray that there may always be room for him in our hearts and
in our homes, for his sake. Amen.

58 O Holy Spirit of God, Teacher, Helper and Friend, open the
hearts and minds of many this Christmastime to the good and
saving news of Jesus Christ, that those who are insecure, or
empty, or aimless, may find in the one from Bethlehem all
that they need today, for his name's sake. Amen.

59 O God our Father, we pray that you will bless every baby
born at Christmastime, their mothers, their families, their
homes. May they receive a better welcome from our world
than Jesus did and may they come to know him as their
Saviour and Friend; for his sake. Amen.

60 Almighty Father, by the glorious incarnation of your Son you
have sent a new light into the world; give us grace that we
may so receive the same light into our hearts as to be guided
by it into the way of everlasting salvation; through the same
Jesus Christ our Lord. Amen.

61 Christ, born in a stable, give courage to the homeless.
Christ who fled to Egypt, comfort the refugee.
Christ who fasted in the desert, have mercy on the hungry.
Christ who hung in torture on the cross, pity those in pain.
Christ who died to save us, above all forgive our sin, our
greed, our selfishness, our unconcern.
Save us today and use us in your loving purposes. Amen.

Before a Carol Service

62 Lord, we have sung these carols and heard this story so many
times before. We confess that we have allowed the most
important event in history to become dulled by familiarity.
Come to us in this act of worship and capture our minds with
truth. May we see the Creator of the universe in a newborn
child. May we worship him with joy.   Amen.

A Bidding Prayer

63 Let us pray for the church: that it may be as humble, as
relevant and as mighty as the Lord who was born of Mary.

Let us pray for the world in all its splendour and need, in
all its grief and its glory: that it may look to God for help.

Let us pray that as God stirred the Wise Men to follow
their star and find the Christ, so may we and all mankind be
stirred to seek for the truth and find the Saviour.

And as God opened the heavens and summoned the
shepherds, let us pray that all men everywhere might look for
God's word and at its coming rise up and go where God shall
direct.

And as God prepared Mary to be the mother of Jesus, let us
ask God to prepare our hearts and the hearts of all people to
receive the Lord of Glory: that in this glad and solemn season
each heart might be a manger and each home a Bethlehem.

A Housewife's Prayer

64 O Lord, as Christmas comes we are busy about many things
in preparation: the making of cakes and puddings; the
anxious search for presents. We have aching hands and feet.
And so we pause and think about the first Christmas when
history turned upon its hinges as your Son became a man,
born into a family, to experience our life and to bear our sin.
Help us to make the real preparations for Christmas by taking
time to contemplate the wonder and the beauty of your Son's
birth, O Lord, and to see our lives in the light of it, for your
tender mercy's sake.   Amen.

65　May our homes be homes of peace and love at Christmas
because we plan carefully, prepare well and give as Jesus
gives, to make it all come true.　Amen.

66　O God, we shall be very busy over Christmas, and we know
we shall be tempted to forget the true meaning of this
festival. Help us to conquer that temptation so that we may
share with our families the true joy of the Saviour's birth, for
his name's sake.　Amen.

Children's Prayers for Christmas

67　Let us thank God for Christmas:
for this happy and exciting time of year.
Thank you, loving Father.
For Christmas trees and decorations.
Thank you, loving Father.
For cards and presents and good food.
Thank you, loving Father.
For fun with family and friends.
Thank you, loving Father.
For singing carols and listening to the Christmas story.
Thank you, loving Father.
For all these things, because we have them to remind us of the
coming of Jesus.
Thank you, loving Father.

68　Let us remember those who do not have the things that make
us happy. In the short time of quiet we shall think of people
whom we know. Then I will say the words: 'As we remember
them', and everyone will reply: 'Help them, loving Father'.

Those who are sad or lonely:
Those who are ill or handicapped:
Those who are poor or hungry:　with no homes/shelter
(Silence)
As we remember them:
help them, loving Father.
Those who are old or unwanted:
(Silence)　Show us ways in which we can help
those for whom we pray.
In J. name.

As we remember them:
help them, loving Father.
Heavenly Father, show us ways in which we may help those
for whom we have prayed; for the sake of Jesus
Christ.   Amen.

69   We thank you, heavenly Father, for sending your only Son
Jesus Christ to become part of the family of man. We thank
you for Mary and Joseph who looked after him and guarded
and protected him when he was little. We thank you for
bringing him to manhood so that in all his earthly life we can
see what you are like. We thank you for reminding us at
Christmas how much you love us and for helping us to realize
that you always have loved us and always will. Help us to love
and serve you gladly in return, through Jesus Christ our
Lord.   Amen.

70   Almighty God, because you sent Jesus to be the Saviour of
mankind, we pray for all the peoples of the world. Because
Jesus was born for all, may he be welcomed by all and may the
love he came to bring strengthen and inspire those who work
to spread his kingdom, for his name's sake.   Amen.

71   We pray, Lord, for all the children in the world who do not
have homes: those who are hungry, sick or sad; all children in
hospital and all whose parents are sick. Bless them and
everybody else who is in trouble and help us all to work
together to make them well and happy again, through the
help of your grace and power, given to the world through
Jesus Christ our Lord.   Amen.

1st Sunday after Christmas
THE INCARNATION

72   Lord, you were born in an overcrowded city, come to our
overcrowded lives. Lord you fill the universe, fill the inner
world of our minds. This we pray, that we may know one

thing, your forgiving love and do one thing, lay our lives at
your feet.   Amen.

73   Lord Jesus Christ, born Jewish and poor, welcomed by
working men and kings, come to our world and heal our deep
divisions. May we who are white and black, female and male,
employer and employed, become children of God, seeing
you, our Lord, in one another.   Amen.

2nd Sunday after Christmas
THE HOLY FAMILY

74   Lord God, whose Son came of age and looked for knowledge
in his Father's house, help us to search for truth where truth is
to be found, to grow in grace as we do your will and to come
to full maturity in Christ, full of grace and truth.   Amen.

75   Lord Jesus, you received gifts from strangers, help us who are
adopted into God's family to obey you as King, to worship
you as Lord, to share in your death and to rejoice with you in
your resurrection.   Amen.

THE EPIPHANY

76   Lord God, we remember how you led the Wise Men to
Bethlehem by the light of a star. Guide us as we travel to the
heavenly city that we and all men may know Jesus as the true
and living way, for his name's sake.   Amen.

77   O Lord, we are called to be your witnesses. Help us to make
Jesus our Saviour known to others through our words and our
lives, our prayers and our gifts, for your sake.   Amen.

78   Heavenly Father, we pray for those who have gone to other
countries with the good news of Jesus. When their work is
difficult and tiring, make them strong; when they are lonely
and homesick, remind them that you are with them; when

they are uncertain what to do, guide them; and keep them at all times loving you, for Jesus' sake.   Amen.

1st Sunday after the Epiphany
THE BAPTISM OF JESUS

79 Lord God, help us who have dipped a foot into the waters of life, to plunge in over our heads, dead to the old ways and fully alive to the new; for the sake of Jesus, who gave his life for those he loved.   Amen.

80 Lord of the church, who baptized us into one body, to share one life and one purpose in the world, deepen our trust in your Spirit, that he may lead us into deeper truth and bring us in love closer to you and to one another.   Amen.

2nd Sunday after the Epiphany
REVELATION: THE FIRST DISCIPLES

81 Lord, you see us busy with our own affairs: break into our lives with your disturbing call and show us what things to abandon and what new things to do, for the sake of him who is worth the loss of all things.   Amen.

82 Lord Jesus, the Good News that comes in person, our encounter with you yesterday has gone like yesterday's news. Meet us today, Lord, and fill us with today's news for today's people, and with that loving invitation to all who look for truth: 'Come and see'.   Amen.

3rd Sunday after the Epiphany
REVELATION: SIGNS OF GLORY

83 Lord God, you have given us a world of natural resources

which fail and run out, a world whose glory fades; renew in us your other gift, Christ himself, the one resource who never fails, the one power in our lives whose product is joy forever.   Amen.

84   Lord, you gave a sign to your people, you drew crowds into the desert to hear the words of eternal life: draw us into your presence daily, to feed, not on present worries and future longings, but on your eternal strength and truth.   Amen.

4th Sunday after the Epiphany
REVELATION: THE NEW TEMPLE

85   Lord, you drove from the temple those whose aim it was to make money; drive from our hearts the desire to own things and to do well in this life. May we, who are your church and temple, be filled with you alone and show your glory to the world.   Amen.

86   Lord, when modern thought and ancient tradition meet to confuse our minds, be our guide; focus the light of your truth not on religious ideas, but on the darker corners of our inner life, that we may be fully open to your presence and may worship you in spirit and in truth.   Amen.

5th Sunday after the Epiphany
REVELATION: PARABLES

87   Lord Jesus, our King and Companion, feed our minds with the right truth at the right time, that our hearts may expand to know you and our lives expand to serve you in your kingdom.   Amen.

88   Lord of light, you alone can resolve the greys of this world into black and white; keep us from judging other people and make us fit for your kingdom.   Amen.

9th Sunday before Easter (Septuagesima)
CHRIST THE TEACHER

89 Jesus our Lord and Teacher, help us to treasure your words, to set them free in the deepest places in our minds, that your strength may free us from our weakness and our lives be full of joy and the power to do your work.   Amen.

90 Lord and Teacher, you leave us free to kill or stunt or choke the living word you sow; help us daily to clear the way for growth, that we may be filled with your abundant life, now and forever.   Amen.

8th Sunday before Easter
CHRIST THE HEALER

91 God of peace and Healer of our troubled consciences, help us to throw away past sins and present comforts, that all our strength may be released for the work your Son has left for us to finish, in his name, the Prince of peace.   Amen.

92 Father, Son and Spirit, Lord of all that is whole, heal the divisions in our personalities; join our doing with our thinking, our feeling with believing, that we may be whole as you are whole, and, living in your presence, find in you our peace.   Amen.

7th Sunday before Easter
CHRIST THE FRIEND OF SINNERS

93 Lord and Father, your Son called the greedy, the selfish and the rejected, who rejoiced in his company; may we who enjoy his presence now go where he would go, for his sake and with the confidence of love.   Amen.

94　Lord and Father, when our sins and failures overwhelm us, and we feel far from your presence, show us the face of Christ, in whom we are forgiven.　Amen.

LENT

A Meditation for Ash Wednesday

95　Help us, O Lord, to fix our minds on the sufferings and temptations of Jesus Christ.

Help us to see him far from home and friends, enduring the trial of his manhood. Help us to see him tortured by hunger, yet not using miraculous powers for selfish ends; desiring the subjection of the world to his Father's will, yet refusing to give honour to the devil; longing to open the eyes of men and women to his glory, yet not stooping to sensational means.

Help us to look steadily at him, who suffered such things for us. Help us to behold his great love. Help us to see his sinless perfection.

When we are in pain or sickness, grief or sorrow, fear or anxiety, help us to turn to him who bore not only pain but also the weight and burden of our sins.

When we seek to conquer sin and bring our lives back into the true and narrow way, help us to turn to him.

At the beginning of this season of Lent, help us now to turn to him.

Holy Jesus, sufferer, sin-bearer, take our hearts and purify them; take our lives and reform them; take all we are this Lent and make us more like you, for your name's sake.　Amen.

For Patience in Seeking God's Will

96　'After fasting for forty days and forty nights, he was hungry' (Matthew 4:2).

Lord we are hungry for the knowledge of the next step we must take. Give us the long patience of Christ that we, like him, may not decide our future in haste. Mercifully grant that hunger for an improvement in our lot, hunger for release from tension, or anxiety, hunger for success in your service, or any other kind of appetite for things hidden in the future, may not stampede the soul into premature decisions.

Save us from turning stones of impatience into the bread of hasty action. May it be our meat and drink to do your will, and like the Saviour find that we have meat to eat we knew not of. Make us not to hunger for tomorrow, but to hunger and thirst after righteousness, in the sure knowledge that in so doing we shall be filled; through Jesus Christ our Lord.   Amen.

97   Help us, Lord, to think about our life as Jesus thought about his: help us to understand the nature of our calling;
    the nature of the One who calls;
    the nature of the world's needs;
    the nature of our own resources;
    the nature of your provision.
Help us not to drift through life but to seek your guidance.

Save us from making hasty decisions; save us from making no decisions at all. Help us to seek not our own glory but yours.

Help us to have no ambition but to do good. Make us pure in heart.

And help us, finally, not to judge ourselves and not to judge others, but to leave judgement where it belongs, with him to whom all power is given, the one who knows all and loves each, Jesus Christ our Saviour and our Lord.   Amen.

98   O Lord Jesus Christ, as man you knew the weakness of our nature and the power of temptation, but overcame all things by the grace of God, so breathe into our hearts the strength of your spirit and clothe us with heavenly armour, that we may conquer all that wars against our souls and may be kept your faithful soldiers and servants to the end.   Amen.

99   Lord Jesus, help us to pray. Increase our faith, that no problem may be too big for us to wrestle with. Help us to see that by keeping us on our knees you are making straight your way and strengthening our trust in your purposes, for your name's sake.   Amen.

Children's Prayers for Lent

100 O God, you made us and you love us: thank you for being so willing to forgive us. Make us quick to own up to you whenever we do wrong so that we may quickly be forgiven. Then our day will not be spoilt by worry and we can be happy all day long, through Jesus Christ our Lord.   Amen.

101 O Lord Jesus Christ, thank you for fasting forty days and forty nights in order to help us. Teach us how to train our bodies to serve our wills and may it always be our will to be your servants, for your dear name's sake.   Amen.

1st Sunday in Lent
THE KING AND THE KINGDOM

102 Lord, you were tested with a choice of three ways to do your work; help us in our own lives always to choose the fourth way, the way of self-giving and of the cross.   Amen.

103 Lord, you have sent us into the world to make followers from every nation; keep us from offering the hungry nothing but bread, from presenting proofs instead of a Person and from serving the forces of this world in the hope that they will serve us, your messengers.   Amen.

2nd Sunday in Lent
THE KING AND THE KINGDOM: CONFLICT

104 Lord, your power to heal was tested against the power which destroys and proved stronger; open our eyes to the signs of your strength in this modern world and open our hearts to the kingdom of God which has come upon us.   Amen.

105 Holy Spirit of God, when evil seems good and good seems evil, come and show us the difference. Holy Giver of life, when we know what is good but cannot follow it, come and give us strength, for the sake of Christ, our Deliverer.   Amen.

3rd Sunday in Lent
THE KING AND THE KINGDOM: SUFFERING

106 Lord Jesus Christ, you died for us; open the inward ear of our minds to hear your voice speaking of the cross, that we who come after you may travel with you and die daily in your service.   Amen.

107 Lord of truth, teach us to live each moment recognizing you as King, so that everywhere we go our words and our working lives make plain the King who suffered and died in love, and rose in power, to bring us to God.   Amen.

4th Sunday in Lent
THE KING AND THE KINGDOM: TRANSFIGURATION

108 Living Lord, you link us with eternity; grant us the vision which passes in a flash but lasts for ever, and grant us all our lives to follow you.   Amen.

109 Loving Father, in our suffering send us strength. Show us the glory at the heart of pain, the glory of Christ, the sufferer who died in love, that we who are freed by his death may freely love him through death to resurrection.   Amen.

5th Sunday in Lent

THE KING AND THE KINGDOM: THE VICTORY OF THE CROSS

110 Father God, you lifted your Son on the cross above all history and raised him from the dead; draw us into his timeless presence; draw us to love him, to leave the sin he has conquered, and to live for him, now and for ever.   Amen.

111 Lord of every power in the universe, who did not resist death on the cross, give us such trust in your victory that we may meet all who choose evil with non-violent love.   Amen.

6th Sunday in Lent

THE KING AND THE KINGDOM: THE WAY OF THE CROSS

112 Lord, you rode straight into the power of the enemy to suffer and die; give us the strength to follow you to the centres of opposition in this world and the confidence which confronts power with love.   Amen.

113 Lord Jesus, King of peace, you led a demonstration: lead us to where true peace lies, not in devotion to law and order, but in taking the way of the cross.   Amen.

For the Sundays in Lent: collects based upon the Gospel readings in the Book of Common Prayer.

1st Sunday in Lent: prayers 102 and 103 above.

2nd Sunday in Lent

114 'A Canaanite woman . . . came to him, crying out, "Lord, have mercy on me! My daughter is suffering terribly . . ."'
(Matthew 15:22).

O Lord, when those we love are attacked by evil, help us never to give up the search for grace and healing, but to spend our lives following you and trusting in your love and power.   Amen.

115 O Lord of all men, sent to your own people but exposed to pressures from strangers, help us when we face demands which lie beyond our limits. Grant us the vision which sees the expanding task and the strength which is able to carry it out, to the glory of your name.   Amen.

116 O Lord, you found faith in unexpected people and those scorned by the religious men of your time. Help us to live in your church so close to those outside it that we may know and share true faith across the border.   Amen.

3rd Sunday in Lent

117 'But if I drive out demons by the finger of God, then the kingdom of God has come to you' (Luke 11:20).

O Lord, whose love has brought us to know you, and whose power drives out the evil inside us, help us to fill our lives with obedience to your will, so that your indwelling may be complete and evil find no home in our hearts; through the power of your Spirit.   Amen.

See also prayer No. 104 above.

4th Sunday in Lent

118 'Jesus then took the loaves, gave thanks, and distributed to those who were seated as much as they wanted' (John 6:11).

O Lord, who used the gift of one to fill the need of thousands, help us so to care for others that without shame or despair we may offer you all we have, to the glory of your name.   Amen.

119 O Lord, you healed the sick and fed the healthy and you know and meet all our needs: keep us from following you merely for the joy and strength you offer; help us in love to take the way of the cross, for your name's sake.   Amen.

5th Sunday in Lent

120 'Jesus said, "Before Abraham was born, I am!" At this, they picked up stones to stone him...' (John 8:58–59).

O Lord, who came to show God to mankind and was not afraid of their anger, take from us the wish to speak in inoffensive whispers in an unwelcoming world and make us strong to speak of you boldly, in your name.   Amen.

121 Lord of all time, you answer our hopes for the future in the present; show us now our King and Deliverer, save us now from our sins, and make us now heirs of the future kingdom, growing like our Lord.   Amen.

Palm Sunday: see prayers 112, 113 and 130

MOTHERING SUNDAY (4th Sunday in Lent)

122 O God of grace and love, in thankfulness for all that you have given us through the loving care and hard work of our mothers, we pray for your richest blessing upon all mothers:
   for those with difficult homes, whose children are more of a problem than a blessing;
   for those with difficult husbands, who find it hard to be constant and loving;
   for those with loved ones far away, and those who are lonely;
   for those who find it hard to make ends meet, or who go short themselves for the sake of their families;
   for those who are nearly at the end of their tether;
   for those mothers who are trying to make Christ real to their families;
   for those who do not know him as their Saviour, nor how to cast their care on him;
   for each one according to her need, hear our prayer and draw all mothers closer to you today, through your Son Jesus Christ our Lord.   Amen.

123 Loving God, we thank you that Jesus enjoyed a mother's love and grew up within a family.

We thank you for the homes where we were born and for the care and affection of our mothers.

We pray for all mothers today:

for expectant mothers, especially those awaiting the birth of their first child;

for those who have young or handicapped children and who get tired and harassed with so much to do;

for those who are anxious because their children are growing up and seem to be growing away from them;

for those who feel a sense of emptiness as their children marry and leave home;

for those who are elderly and may feel unwanted;

for those who have no husband to share their responsibilities—the widowed, the divorced, and the unmarried mothers.

We pray also for those who have been denied the privilege of motherhood—those who cannot have children of their own and those who have never had the opportunity to marry.

Finally we pray for those who are closest to us: may we love and care for them as we ourselves have been loved and helped. We ask it for your love's sake. Amen.

124 Remember, O Lord, all those in need: people with no good food or proper clothes; no home of their own or no work to do; no family or friends, or no knowledge of your love. Supply their needs. Bless those who try to help them and bring them all to trust in you. Amen.

125 We thank you, heavenly Father, for our friends and families. May your love surround them; may your strength protect them; may your truth guide them; that we may love one another very much, and love you with all our hearts, and best of all; for Jesus' sake. Amen.

126 We pray to you, O God, that husbands and wives may love and serve each other; that fathers and mothers may be fair and kind to their children; that sons and daughters may obey and

help their parents; that brothers and sisters may share willingly and give generously; and that all of us may grow daily more like Jesus Christ, who once gave himself for us and is now the best friend of every family; for his name's sake. Amen.

A Responsive Prayer

127 As people who belong to God:
>   *we must be patient, humble and kind;*
forbearing and forgiving one another:
>   *as the Lord has forgiven us.*
Above all we must have love:
>   *which binds us together in harmony.*
Let the peace of Christ rule in our lives:
>   *as we join in worshipping him.*
Our songs and hymns are full of praise.
>   *giving thanks to God through Christ.*
Our work and service is whole-hearted:
>   *not just for one another, but for Christ.*
So that in every word and deed:
>   *our aim may be to please and honour him.*

Amen.

A Children's Prayer for Mothering Sunday

128 Loving Father, thank you for our homes and for family life.

Today we thank you especially for the love and care of our mothers.

If we have no mother of our own we thank you for whoever takes her place.

We thank you that she cooks our meals, cleans the house, and mends our clothes.

We thank you that she corrects us when we are naughty and cheers us up when we feel sad.

We are sorry when we forget that housework can make her tired.

We are sorry if our carelessness causes her extra work.

We are sorry if we sometimes seem to be ungrateful for all that she does for us.

Help us to be more thoughtful, helpful and kind at home;
through Jesus Christ our Lord. Amen.

A Children's Prayer for Father's Day

129 Loving God, there are so many things for which we are
grateful.
We are especially thankful today for our fathers.
We thank you for their love, care and protection.
We thank you that they work to earn money to buy us food
and clothes and all we need.
We thank you that they play with us and take us on
holiday.
We remember those who have no father and ask that there
may be someone who will look after them and make them
happy.
Lord we are glad to remember that Jesus taught us that we
can call you 'Father'. Help us to try to please you as
well. Amen.

PRAYERS FOR HOLY WEEK

Palm Sunday

130 Come into our city, Lord, and bring hope and a reason for joy.
Ride into the hopelessness and fear in which so many people
still live their lives.
> *All:* *Blessed be the King, who comes in the name of the*
> *Lord.*
Come into our temple, Lord and cleanse it of all that is not in
accordance with your will and your way. Stride into this
place, Lord and challenge it with the purity of your life and
the power of your presence.
> *All:* *Blessed be the King who comes in the name of the*
> *Lord.*
Sit with us, Lord, and teach us your truth. Be patient with
our inability and unwillingness to learn from you. Give to us

a fresh vision of your purpose and lead us out of darkness into
light.

> *All:*   *Blessed be the King, who comes in the name of the
> Lord.*

As you entered your city and your temple, O Lord, so enter
into our hearts and minds this day. Help us to welcome you
with truth and with integrity and teach us to walk in your
way all the days of our life; through the same Jesus Christ our
Lord. Amen.

Maundy Thursday (The Garden of Gethsemane)

131 In a garden open to the skies Jesus prays for strength to face
the pain and suffering of the cross. With the stars above him,
and the hard earth beneath him, he surrenders his will to the
will of his Father.

> *All:*   *Your will be done on earth as it is in heaven.*

On a hillside Jesus sweats blood and wrestles with all his
might. The disciples to whom he looks for support are unable
to bear it. They find escape in sleep.

> *All:*   *Your will be done on earth as it is in heaven.*

Into the garden, under the darkening sky, comes Judas with
the soldiers. The Prince of peace is surrounded by men of war;
the God of love is encircled with hate; the Man who embraced
the sick and the outcast is kissed by a traitor.

> *All:*   *Lead us not into temptation, but deliver us from evil.*

Good Friday

132 Jesus was crucified as a common criminal, the victim of
political intrigue and religious bigotry. He did all that was
good and was killed by all that was evil.

> *All:*   *Father, forgive us.*

Jesus was reviled as a failure; laughed at as a fool; scorned for
his gentleness and meekness and put to death for his
goodness.

> *All:*   *Father, forgive us.*

Jesus died and men still die. War and bloodshed still go on;
men are tortured and crucified by religious and political

fanatics. We recall the crucifixion of Christ and the sacrifices which men and women are still called upon to make.

All: Father, forgive us.

The Crowd

133 Have mercy, O Lord, on all those whose judgement of truth is rooted in the opinion of others; all who are swayed by pressure groups, to do deeds which they themselves would never think of doing; all whose lack of purpose, lack of conviction, lack of stability, or lack of employment, makes them available to the purposes of others and delivers them as a weapon into the hands of evil men. Give to all people everywhere, O Lord, a spirit of responsibility and discernment, and make them more ready to seek for the truth, and less ready to believe a lie; through Jesus Christ our Lord.   Amen.

The High Priest

134 Have mercy, O Lord, on all who bear high office and abuse its authority; all who plot courses of political action for the sole purpose of protecting their own positions; all who persecute prophets because of the evil they expose; all who manufacture a lie for public consumption; all who treat prophets and public alike as pawns and puppets: on all such, everywhere, O Lord, have mercy. Help them to worship truth and to give God the glory. Teach them to know and to understand, to believe and to trust, that for the mighty as for the meek it is only by losing our life that we find it, only by dying that we live, only by following Christ that we lead men: for his name's sake.   Amen.

Pilate

135 Have mercy, O Lord, on all who are called to the terrible loneliness of giving judgement; all who know that upon their conclusions rest the lives of others; all who are the object of bribery or menace. Give them great courage and great

goodness. Make them wise in heart, humble in spirit, accurate in thought, brave in decision, resolute in life. Make them righteous and give them peace, through Jesus Christ our Lord.   Amen.

Frightened Disciples

136 O God, you know our weakness: have mercy on us and on all Christian people when we are tempted to cast away our confidence in Christ. When the high and mighty are against him and when the crowd cries for his blood, help us to cling to his cross and behold his face. And as you saved and delivered the first disciples, so, by the power of the resurrection, save and deliver us too, we pray, through the same Jesus Christ our Lord.   Amen.

Barabbas

137 Have mercy, O Lord, on all who have killed and robbed and destroyed, but go unpunished. Turn their hearts, O Lord, and help them to repent. By the wounds of Christ save them from the wounds of fruitless remorse. Give them instead that godly sorrow which leads to life. And may lives which have been slaves to evil become servants of love, through Jesus Christ our Lord.   Amen.

Joseph of Arimathea

138 Bless all, O Lord, who worship you in secret: all whose hearts are growing round an undeclared allegiance; all whose life is laden with a treasure they would pour out at your feet; all who know with greater certainty each day that they have found the pearl of greatest price. Then, by the power of the cross, O Christ, claim your victory in their heart and lead them to the liberty of being seen by all men to be yours, for your dear name's sake.   Amen.

Children's Prayers for Holy Week

139 Thank you, Lord, for sending your Son Jesus Christ into the world so that by coming to know him we might also come to know you. Thank you, Lord Jesus, for going to Jerusalem as a King and for making people take sides either for you or against. Thank you for going to the cross to show us how great a difference there is between serving and not serving you. Thank you for dying there to save us. Heavenly Father, help us this week to remember that even when men were plotting to take his life Jesus spent his time in loving and serving other people. Help us this week to love and serve him more, for his dear sake.   Amen.

140 We thank you, Lord God, for the goodness of Jesus: we open our hearts to him so that he may dwell within us and make us good. We thank you, Lord God, for the courage of Jesus: help us like him to stand up for what is right and true. We thank you, Lord God, for the first disciples who learned to love Jesus and who taught others to love him too: help us, like them, to spread the knowledge of his love. Help us, during this Holy Week, to think carefully about what Jesus did on the last days before his crucifixion. Help us to understand what happened and why it happened. Prepare us to understand more about why Jesus died, and help us to know that he died for each one of us. Help us to see more clearly the power of his resurrection and to share in it by giving our lives to him, for his dear name's sake.   Amen.

141 Jesus Christ, when you were born the stable was cold and dirty; during your life you suffered rejection from those who ought to have known better; on Good Friday it was grim and dark. And all this was for me. Thank you, Lord.   Amen.

142 Heavenly Father, we thank you for giving your Son to die on the cross that we might be forgiven. Help us to understand the extent of our sin and the greatness of his love, so that we may trust him as our Saviour and serve him as our Lord.   Amen.

143 Heavenly Father, there are many roads by which men seek for truth, and their hearts are only at rest when they find you. The road to life is the one that leads to a cross. Help us to lose our life in this world so that we may find it in you and accept your offer of company along the way, through Jesus Christ our Lord. Amen.

GOOD FRIDAY

The Seven Words from the Cross

144 'Father, forgive them, for they do not know what they are doing' (Luke 23:34).

Let us pray for all those who are doing evil. Let us pray for all proud, violent and malicious men; let us pray for blasphemers, unbelievers, heretics; let us pray for all who exploit their fellow men, tyrannize them, use them as pawns in political power struggles. Let us pray for all who abuse power, and so betray the trust placed in them. Let us pray for all who persecute Christians for their faith. Let us pray for the church when it is tempted to put expediency before truth, self interest before love, and for the sake of winning human praise, crucifies the Lord afresh. Let us pray for ourselves when lack of zeal, the deceitfulness of riches and the cares of this world make us the sleeping partners of social evil. 'Father forgive us for we know not what we do.'

'Today you will be with me in paradise' (Luke 23:43).

Let us pray for all those who want to repent and begin a new life, but who feel that it is too late. Let us pray that they may learn from the dying thief that Christ is the one nearest to them and that paradise is as close as he is. And let us, as one with the thief, pray as he did: 'Lord remember me.' So may our last hour blend into the light of paradise, through the power of the crucified.

'I am thirsty' (John 19:28).

Let us pray for all who suffer physical distress through lack of food and water and for those whose bodies are not able to benefit from the abundance of food near at hand. Let us pray that in their hearts they may find rivers of living water to refresh and sustain them and prepare the way for physical relief and healing. And let us pray for all who hunger and thirst after righteousness; that in their obedience to Christ they might have meat to eat unknown to them before, and, according to Christ's promise, be satisfied.

'Mother, there is your son. Son, there is your mother.'

Let us pray for family ties. Let us pray for the bereaved; let us pray that Christ may create relationships which survive the worst blows which life can give. And let us thank him for his power in creating new relationships which sustain us in the different stages of our pilgrimage.

'My God, my God, why have you forsaken me?'
(Matthew 27:46).

Let us pray for all who are forsaken; for nations which are forsaken; for children who are forsaken; for old people who are forsaken; for prisoners and captives who are forsaken; for prophets and idealists who are forsaken; and for ourselves when we feel ourselves to be forsaken. May we and all men everywhere find within God's absolute demand his ultimate succour and understand that below the level of the deepest sorrows are the everlasting arms of his healing love. May we learn to say, 'I shall yet give thanks to him who is my Saviour, my King and my God.'

'It is finished' (John 19:30).

Let us thank Christ for finishing the work that he came to do; let us thank him for having done all that is necessary for our salvation; let us thank him that because his work is finished our search for forgiveness is finished and our striving for pardon is finished. And let us thank God that with the end of our search there is the beginning of a life of thankfulness, praise and service, offered to God not from fear but out of love. Let us pray that we may find the work that he has for us to do and finish it.

'Father, into your hands I commit my spirit' (Luke 23:46).

Let us thank God that when the conscious control of our life is beyond our grasp we may still repose upon God's eternal changelessness. Teach us, O Lord, to fear the grave as little as we fear our bed; and fill our lives with the hope and faith of the resurrection, in the knowledge that in death our lives pass into the hands which made the world and guide the universe, the hands of the almighty Creator. And may we place our lives in those hands while life is strong and full and sweet. Father, with thanksgiving, into your hands we commit our spirit.   Amen.

A Children's Prayer

145 Jesus said, 'Greater love has no-one than this, that one lay down his life for his friends' (John 15:13).

Let us thank God for sending his son Jesus into our world. Let us think of Jesus and pray that we may be more like him. As we remember his kindness in healing and helping, we know that we too should be kind.
Lord, make us more like Jesus.
As we remember his courage in facing his enemies, we know that we should be brave.
Lord, make us more like Jesus.
As we remember how he forgave those who put him to death, we know that we should be forgiving.
Lord, make us more like Jesus.
As we remember his love in laying down his life, we know that we should be loving.
Lord, make us more like Jesus.
Lord God, we are sorry that Jesus was killed. But we thank you that in this way you have shown how much you love us. Although we think of his suffering today, we are also glad to remember that he conquered death and came back alive to be with his disciples and with us for ever.   Amen.

Good Friday Evening

146 Lord, it is hard to concentrate our thoughts for very long on what happened nearly two thousand years ago. Somehow the cross on the hill seems remote from the fireside we have left and to which we shall return. Yet the sins of those who crucified Jesus are our sins. Our needs are the needs of all mankind. Help us tonight to see the cross, eternal, not only in the heart of God but in the hearts of us men and women. So may we receive your forgiveness and your peace, through Jesus Christ our Lord.   Amen.

EASTER

147 Living God, the resurrection of Jesus throws wide the door between ourselves and life eternal. We go through that door today, inheriting from Christ the ambition to serve you totally and to spread your kingdom. Give us, we pray, the power to turn thought into action and ambition into achievement, through Jesus Christ our Lord.   Amen.

148 Lord and Father, send your spirit into your worldwide church, that those who approach it in sadness and despair may find the gloriously living body of Christ and all may believe.   Amen.

149 Lord God, you freed Christ from death once for all time; free us each day from our old self, that we may live the new life of Christ now and for ever.   Amen.

150 O Christ, you lived to show what life is like, and died to show that sin is death; you rose to raise us up to life eternal. Help us to follow you and love you forever.   Amen.

151 Father, we thank you that in finding you we also find new friends and the happiness of much love. When we have entered into this fellowship help us to give ourselves to it, and welcome others into it, through Jesus Christ our Lord.   Amen.

152 Your will, O God, is our peace. Help us to want for ourselves the things you want us to have. Help us to love your programme for living. Help us to welcome your orders for the day. For when these prayers are answered our heart will find its home, in Jesus Christ our Lord. Amen.

153 Loving Father, help us to abandon that love of self which leads to death and enable us to cause that kind of self esteem itself to die; help us to be willing to die to self. Then, Lord, help us to live to Christ and grant us the power of the life he came to bring; for his name's sake. Amen.

154 Lord Jesus, our risen Saviour, we rejoice in your mighty victory over sin and death. You are the Prince of life: you are alive for evermore. Help us to know your presence, not only as we worship you here, but at home, and at work, and wherever we go; for your great name's sake. Amen.

155 Lord Jesus, set our hearts on fire with your love that with joy and thankfulness in our hearts we may walk once again on your royal road, inspired by the message of the cross and the joy of Easter Day. Amen.

156 Risen Lord, our Bringer-back from death, save us from standing between you and our neighbours and hiding you from their sight by lack of love. May we and all your people show that you are not a prisoner of the past but alive in the world today, and may all hungry hearts find purpose and new life in you, Creator infinite, blessed for ever. Amen.

157 Lord, we do not always find it easy to recognize your coming to us. Therefore when our spirits are downcast and we believe that you have failed, reveal yourself to us afresh: open our eyes to undiscovered secrets of your word; meet us in the breaking of the bread; set our heavy hearts on fire with love and send us on our way rejoicing; for your great name's sake. Amen.

158 Our Lord and God, forgive the doubting heart in each of us, which questions your resurrection. We are men of our age

and want to see and touch before we believe. And yet we thank you for that blessing, reserved for those who do not see and yet believe. Grant us the faith which looks to Jesus, risen from the dead, our Saviour and our living Lord.   Amen.

159 Sometimes, Lord, you seem to us as a stranger on the shore. Then you remind us of our calling: challenge us with hard commandments, draw out our trust and when we obey, you reveal yourself, not as a stranger, but as a friend. Help us to discover you again today, as we do what you tell us, for your name's sake.   Amen.

160 As your children, Lord, we should not be afraid. And yet we are afraid: of people we work with, of neighbours, even of our own families. Our faith is behind the locked doors of our hearts. And yet, O Lord, you come with peace and the coming is enough to fill our heart with joy. Unlock our heart from within and send us on your errands, your message not only in our hearts but on our lips, for your name's sake.   Amen.

161 We thank you, Lord Jesus, for your last words. We treasure them for the promise of your Holy Spirit to give us power. Help us now to obey your command to be witnesses to the ends of the earth, starting from where we are now; for your name's sake.   Amen.

162 Full authority in heaven and on earth is given to you, Lord Jesus Christ. Give us, we pray, such a sense of your power that we gladly obey your will. Make us disciples in all nations. Make us messengers to all people. And we thank you that your presence will be with us this day, wherever we go, in your name.   Amen.

163 We thank you, Lord, that you did not leave us without your blessing. You have put a new song on our lips, and a new joy in our hearts. We praise you for a risen Saviour; we rejoice in a living Lord, and we offer our lives today in thankful sacrifice to Jesus Christ our Lord.   Amen.

164 We thank you, Father, for every Christian who bears witness
to the risen power of Jesus Christ. We have not seen as the
apostles have seen, but we have met him in our lives. That
meeting has changed us and we shall never be the same again.
Help us to be faithful ambassadors that others may meet him,
to the glory of Christ and the salvation of man.   Amen.

165 Risen Lord, we thank you for the varied and vivid accounts   𝘹
given to us by those who actually talked with you and ate
with you and touched you. We thank you for this visible and
physical evidence given to them of your power over death.
And we thank you for the invisible, spiritual evidence which
each of us can experience in the heart, declaring to us that
Christ is still alive. May we, like the first disciples, be brave
enough to tell what we have seen and heard, so that others
may enjoy the friendship which we have with you and which
is our greatest blessing: for your dear name's sake.   Amen.

166 Almighty God, our Father, we have seen you in the changed
lives of the disciples, and in the growth of the church from   𝘹
eleven men in Jerusalem to a world-wide fellowship: but
sometimes we still doubt.

   In our own day we have seen missionaries leave all to follow
you: but sometimes we still doubt.

   We have seen confirmed sceptics changed into
compassionate Christians: but sometimes we still doubt.

   We have seen the burning joy of men and women who have
survived torture and persecution for their faith: but
sometimes we still doubt.

   Father, use each experience of doubt to build up our faith.
You do not call us to blind belief, but to a faith we can prove
through the help of your Holy Spirit. May we persevere in
looking for answers in the right places and from the right
people; through Jesus Christ our Lord.   Amen.

A Litany of the Resurrection

167 We confess, O Lord, that death is the great enemy in our life,

so strong that it is hard to believe that Jesus is not buried in
Palestine.

> *The angel said, 'He is not here;*
> *he has risen!'*

We envy those who saw him face to face and feel for Thomas
in his doubt. And yet we know he lives.

> *Blessed are those who have not seen*
> *and yet have believed.*

In the world we know we should be bold in the Master's
service but we find ourselves fearful and ill equipped.

> *Jesus said, 'You will receive power*
> *when the Holy Spirit comes on you.'*

We would prefer to be quiet Christians. The responsibility of
making Jesus known is a heavy one.

> *Jesus said, 'You will be my witnesses*
> *to the ends of the earth.'*

We are disciples of the Lord. We commit ourselves to his
service and in his risen power resolve to make him known by
the way we live and by the words we speak for overwhelming
victory is ours through him who loved us, even Jesus Christ
our Saviour.   Amen.

Meditation

168   At the root of life and interwoven in its suffering and dying,
loving and creating, there is bread. And Jesus took this and
blessed and broke it, and said: 'This is my body which is
given for you. Do this in remembrance of me.'

We thank you, Lord Jesus, for your body, our bread, freely
offered to release us from the power of sin. We thank you for
this simple sign to remember you by. In the breaking of
bread give strength for our bodies and strength for our souls
each day to do your will until you return in your
glory.   Amen.

Children's Prayers for Easter

169   O God our Father, we thank you for this happy day. Thank
you for Easter eggs and cards and for our being on holiday.

We thank you because these things remind us of the true
meaning of Easter.
We remember with gladness:
that Jesus overcame death and showed himself to his friends:
we praise you, we thank you.
That he is alive for evermore:
we praise you, we thank you.
That he is with us now to be our friend:
we praise you, we thank you.
That he will be with us always, to the end of time:
we praise you, we thank you.
Thank you, Lord God, for the good news of Easter.   Amen.

170   When we feel sad or worried; when we are frightened or
lonely:
help us to know you are near us.
When our friends go against us; when people make us
annoyed:
help us to know you are near us.
When work seems hard or dull; when we need help to keep us
from doing wrong:
help us to know you are near us.
When everything is going well and when we are full of
happiness:
help us to know you are near us.
Lord Jesus, help us to know that nothing can ever separate us
from your love.   Amen.

1st Sunday after Easter

THE UPPER ROOM:
THE BREAD OF LIFE

171   Lord Jesus, you died for us and found your peace in doing the
Father's will: give us the strength to go into all the world
ready to receive wounds such as yours, that others may know
your peace and your salvation.   Amen.

172 Father God, grant us the twin gifts of obedience and love,
that we may in love lay our lives at your feet and in obedience
take your love to others, through the one who loved us and
made us free, Jesus Christ our Saviour. Amen.

2nd Sunday after Easter

THE EMMAUS ROAD:
THE GOOD SHEPHERD

173 Lord, your followers recognized you in the breaking of bread:
grant us the same power that we may know the same joy and
grant us the same unity that we may spread the same
faith. Amen.

174 Lord, you lead your followers through death to resurrection:
help us daily to listen to your voice and to lay down our lives
for you as you laid down your life for us. Amen.

3rd Sunday after Easter

THE LAKESIDE:
THE RESURRECTION AND THE LIFE

175 God of life and truth, help us to grasp the evidence of those
who saw and heard and touched our risen Lord and help us
like them to follow him to death. Amen.

176 Lord, your love brought Lazarus from the tomb: bring your
church into the light of day to live and work for you, that
faith may come to life in those who see our
resurrection. Amen.

4th Sunday after Easter
THE CHARGE TO PETER:
THE WAY, THE TRUTH, AND THE LIFE

177 Lord of love, you gave your life for your sheep: send us leaders who have given their lives to you, who are filled with love for you alone, that we may be fed the words of eternal life and be one flock, following you forever.   Amen.

178 Lord Jesus, you came in love to heal the blind, the deaf and the dying, open our eyes to the way and our ears to the truth, that our lives may be spent spreading the Good News we have seen and heard until you come again in power to judge the world.   Amen.

179 Jesus, the Way, direct me; Jesus, the Truth, instruct me; Jesus, the Life, empower me so that each day I may walk in your way, study your word and do your will, for your great name's sake.   Amen.

5th Sunday after Easter
GOING TO THE FATHER

180 Lord, you returned to the Father by way of the cross: when we fear for the future show us the path of love and lead us a step at a time until you receive us in your Father's house.   Amen.

181 Lord, you see time whole where we see only part of the present and part of the past: help us to understand your words, and bring us through puzzlement, doubt and sadness into the joy of your presence for ever.   Amen.

ASCENSION DAY

182 Help us Lord, to understand the meaning of the Ascension. Help us to accept, in all its wonder, the glorious fact of your

life on earth and may our vision of it become fuller and
sharper every day, so may we share the blessings of your first
disciples.

Help us to accept your going from the world and to
understand it not as deprivation but as the pathway to power
unlimited by time and space.

Help us to look for your coming, not in flesh that we see and
touch, but by your dwelling in the brotherhood and by your
Spirit in our mind and heart and soul.

And by the gift of that same Spirit, Lord, help us to live a life
on earth which will give to all men everywhere a full, clear
vision of your grace and truth, your beauty and your reality,
here and now, until you come at the end of the ages as Judge
and King, O Lord, the same yesterday, today and
forever.   Amen.

183 Lord, we thank you that you ascended as King of heaven and
earth and that you are in control of all things. Help us to trust
you when life is difficult and obey you at all times. We ask
this for the honour of your name.   Amen.

184 Jesus, our Teacher and example, you trained your disciples
for their task then left them to experience the coming of your
Spirit: help missionaries to know how to teach and to train
others and to know when to hand over the work and move
out, that the Spirit may come and your church may grow, for
your great name's sake.   Amen.

Sunday after Ascension Day
THE ASCENSION OF CHRIST

185 Lord God, send your love into our hearts, that we may gladly
go into the world which Christ has left and spread the good
news of his kingdom in the power which he has given
us.   Amen.

186 Father God, as there is one Christ in heaven, make us one body on earth, that we may do the will of our Lord and Head in the joy of unity and make him known throughout the world.   Amen.

PENTECOST

Luke 4:18–19

187 May the Spirit of the Lord be upon us that we may announce good news to the poor, proclaim release for the prisoners, and recovery of sight for the blind; that we may let the broken victim go free and proclaim the year of the Lord's favour; according to the example of Christ and by his grace.   Amen.

Isaiah 11:2

188 Grant us, Lord, the spirit of wisdom and insight, the spirit of counsel and power, the spirit of knowledge and of the fear of the Lord; to make us quick in understanding and true in judgement; according to the example of Christ and by his grace.   Amen.

Acts 2

189 Bless us, Lord, when we are all together with one consent in one place and grant that in our common life we may know the coming of your Spirit. Make our hearts as one and clothe our minds with fire; then make us, Lord, separately and together, preachers of your good news whom all the world shall hear and understand; through Jesus Christ our Lord.   Amen.

Galatians 5:22–24

190 Grant to us Lord, the fruit of the Spirit: and may your life in ours fulfil itself in love, joy, peace; patience, kindness, goodness; faithfulness, gentleness and self-control. May our lower nature, with its passions and desires, be crucified with

Christ, that true life may come. And may the Holy Spirit, the source of that new life, direct its course to your glory, through Jesus Christ our Lord.   Amen.

191 We thank you, God our Father, for sending your Holy Spirit to guide and strengthen us, to help us understand the Bible, and to love and serve the Lord Jesus; for his sake.   Amen.

192 We praise you, O God, because you gave the Holy Spirit to the first Christians. You made Jesus real to them, you taught them the truth and gave them power to witness boldly. Fill us with the same spirit that we may know their experience and follow their example, for Jesus' sake.   Amen.

193 Lord Jesus Christ, we close our minds against a threatening world because we are afraid. Cross our barricades and enter our lives that we may know your peace and go out to bring it to others.   Amen.

194 God of an explosive world, where bombs and weapons talk, send into our hearts the dynamite of your Spirit, that we may know power and peace together and speak of you to all people in ways which reach the centre of their being.   Amen.

195 When people are all around us, Lord, and we see their unseeing eyes and know them to be lost in their private world, unable to see a sparrow die, Lord help us to communicate. By your Spirit break through the barriers of men's minds and help us to help each other with the gospel of the risen Lord, for his name's sake.   Amen.

196 Living Lord, traveller in the way of men, our trail blazer into eternity, kindle in our hearts the passionate fire of heaven; burn from our minds the cancer of selfish thought. So may we dare to imitate your love, and risking all through your emboldening, dare to share your truth at all times and in all ways, bringing glory to your name, now and forever.   Amen.

197 Heavenly Father, who sent your anointing Spirit upon your
Son that he might be the instrument of your healing grace:
send anew your Spirit upon us, that we may proclaim in word
and deed the liberty and healing of your gospel: we ask this
through Jesus Christ, our Lord.   Amen.

198 We thank you, Holy Spirit, for your renewing power; for
your life, your gifts, your fruits; for the freedom and the joy
which you bring; for the community of love which you create;
and for your faithful abiding with us always: to the glory of
God the Father, through the mediation of Jesus Christ, his
Son, our Lord.   Amen.

199 Your Spirit, O God, came to the disciples through Jesus
Christ our Lord: bless your disciples today with the same gift
from the same Master, that they may find fullness of life in
him, and serve him with joy and power all the days of their
life, for his truth and mercy's sake.   Amen.

200 Father, by your Spirit, teach us more about Jesus. Make us
eager to learn. Stimulate our minds that we may reason with
you; enliven our imaginations and expand our
understanding; guide our emotions and shape our reactions
according to your wholesome intentions; and as we yield our
wills to your care, inspire us to a genuine commitment to do
only such things as will please you. And in every
circumstance of life sustain our determination to glorify you,
through Jesus Christ our Lord.   Amen.

201 Help us, Lord, to accept you, to acknowledge you, to let you
loose in our lives. Help us to give you the centre, the
circumference, the radius and the run of our lives. Be the
object of our faith, the reason for our hope and the origin of
our love; through Jesus Christ our Lord.   Amen.

202 **A Children's Prayer for Whitsun**

We remember today how the coming of God's Holy Spirit on
the day of Pentecost changed the lives of the disciples.

Loving Lord God, thank you for the joy of the disciples. We
need the gift of joy:
give us your Spirit, Lord.
Thank you for the courage of your disciples. We need the gift
of courage:
give us your Spirit, Lord.
Thank you for the goodness and unselfishness of the disciples.
We need these gifts:
give us your Spirit, Lord.
Thank you for the way the disciples spread the good news of
your love. We need to be your messengers:
give us your Spirit, Lord.

203 God our Father, you seek men and women to worship you in
spirit and in truth. We ask you to inspire and bless the
worship of this church in words and music, prayers and
hymns, psalms and lessons. Open the hearts and lips of those
who worship you today all over the world, that all of us may
listen with an alert conscience to the preaching of your word
and come to receive the sacrament with true repentance and
faith. We ask this in the name of him, through whom alone
our worship is acceptable to you, our Lord and Saviour, Jesus
Christ.   Amen.

TRINITY SUNDAY

204 Almighty God, grant to all Christians everywhere a new
understanding of your kingdom, a new knowledge of your
power, a fresh vision of your glory; and so awaken us to the
reality of your presence that we may be caught up in your
purposes and serve you with a burning spirit and a quiet
mind, through Jesus Christ our Lord.   Amen.

205 God of all knowledge, beyond the reach of those who would
stand and wait for proof, help us to do the will of Christ, and
come to know you in him.   Amen.

206 Lord, keep our lives simple in a complex world and help us to live by the single rule of love, that all the universe may be reunited with its Maker.   Amen.

A Children's Prayer

207 Holy Father God, all the universe belongs to you. We worship you because you are the Lord of the world, the stars and space. We praise you because you have made everything so wonderfully. We give you thanks because we know that every good thing comes from you. We know that you are all goodness, that you are a holy God.

We are sorry for those times when we fail to be good. Help us to know you will forgive us and help us to be better. We come now to worship you in the beauty of holiness.   Amen.

2nd Sunday after Pentecost (Trinity 1)
THE PEOPLE OF GOD: THE CHURCH'S UNITY

208 God of the living, prune from our lives all weak, diseased and useless growth and keep our thoughts and actions rooted in our Lord, that love and joy may multiply in our lives and in the world, to your glory.   Amen.

209 Lord, teach us to pray and send your Spirit to graft us together, living cells growing in truth and love, that we may be in the world a unity, the living and the growing body of Christ, our Lord and Head.   Amen.

3rd Sunday after Pentecost (Trinity 2)
THE LIFE OF THE BAPTIZED: THE CHURCH'S CONFIDENCE IN CHRIST

210 Lord, if we leave your presence, we leave life itself; keep us in

your love and truth and feed us daily with the word of life, for the sake of your glory in the world.   Amen.

211   Lord, forgive us when we despair; when evil seems stronger than good, and death is permanent and life has lost its meaning. Do not turn us out of your presence, but show us, as never before, the power of your resurrection.   Amen.

4th Sunday after Pentecost (Trinity 3)

THE FREEDOM OF THE SONS OF GOD: THE CHURCH'S MISSION TO THE INDIVIDUAL

212   Lord Jesus, you died in love and rose in power, transplant in us a new heart of love and send us out new people, strong to heal others by the power which healed us, free to lay down our lives in love.   Amen.

213   Lord Jesus, you came to look for the lost and live with the rejected: breathe into us your love and compassion, that we may live as you lived and rate your joy in heaven above our image on earth.   Amen.

5th Sunday after Pentecost (Trinity 4)

THE NEW LAW: THE CHURCH'S MISSION TO ALL MEN

214   Lord, save us from the sorrow of keeping our possessions and losing you. Keep before us a vision of your love, the love which makes all things possible, even our free response to your death on the cross.   Amen.

215   Send us, Holy Spirit of God, to speak where we may be heard, and to live where we may be seen, that Christ may be known today in the place where all things happen, in the heart of this modern age.   Amen.

6th Sunday after Pentecost (Trinity 5)
THE NEW MAN

216 Father God, you gave us the world and we have wasted it and
used its resources selfishly: show us the way back to a new
beginning, come in love to meet us, and make us a new
people fit for a new heaven and a new earth.   Amen.

217 Lord, when we are strangers alone in the crowd, call us into
your presence and make us whole; restore our minds and
bodies, and restore our love for people, that we may be fully
alive to others and fully alive to you.   Amen.

7th Sunday after Pentecost (Trinity 6)
THE MORE EXCELLENT WAY

218 Lord God, you loved the world at the cost of sending your
Son: send us your measureless love, that we may forgive other
people with no thought of the cost, for the sake of the One who
died and rose again for our forgiveness.   Amen.

219 Lord, you sent your Son to bring us life: send us your Spirit of
love, which binds us to live as Christ lived and frees us to give
our time and our money, our present and our future, to our
neighbour, for your sake.   Amen.

8th Sunday after Pentecost (Trinity 7)
THE FRUIT OF THE SPIRIT

220 Lord Jesus, your love generates love: send us your Spirit, and
send us where wrong breeds wrong, to break the cycle of evil
as you broke it once for all, by love crucified.   Amen.

221 Lord Jesus, killed by hate and raised by love, help us to be
your witnesses in a hostile world; to show most love where

there is most hate and to live united to one another until you come again.   Amen.

9th Sunday after Pentecost (Trinity 8)
THE WHOLE ARMOUR OF GOD

222 Lord, you care for all our needs, send us faith that we, who think our problems are great, may trust in that which is greater, your everlasting power and mercy.   Amen.

Prayer 213 is also suitable here.

10th Sunday after Pentecost (Trinity 9)
THE MIND OF CHRIST

223 Lord, make us a community where each one loves the others and all are happy to take the lowest place, that in living as you lived we may turn our competitive world upside down, for the sake of your love.   Amen.

224 Lord, save us from despair, the despair of knowing the inner depths of our minds, the depth of our sin; show us the matching depths of your forgiveness and fill us with the love which reaches every corner of the universe.   Amen.

11th Sunday after Pentecost (Trinity 10)
THE SERVING COMMUNITY

225 Lord, you loved us, and love took you to the cross; help us to take the path of love and suffering, always putting the good of others above our own, for the sake of your love and in the power of your resurrection.   Amen.

226 Lord Jesus Christ, in your kingdom the same pay for everybody is unknown, but the great gift of salvation is given

to all. Give us also such joy in serving you and in serving one another that differentials are forgotten and God dwells in us as we love one another.   Amen.

12th Sunday after Pentecost (Trinity 11)
THE WITNESSING COMMUNITY

227 Father God, whose glory left the temple and shone from the cross; send us out from our churches into your world; to be one body living for you, suffering for you and making your glory visible to men.   Amen.

228 Lord of joy, we bring you our sadness; Lord of peace, we bring you our troubled minds; Lord of light, we bring you our lives shadowed by selfishness; light us with your presence and send us out to light the world.   Amen.

13th Sunday after Pentecost (Trinity 12)
THE SUFFERING COMMUNITY

229 Lord, your love goes beyond death and beyond suffering; help us to love one another beyond all reasonable bounds, to explore the meaning of the universe by dying for one another and so to come to our eternal home.   Amen.

230 Lord God, who sent the Prince of peace into a violent world to be killed; send us out into our world of wealth, hunger and self-regard, that men may explore the limits of Christ's love as we live and die for others, in the power of your Spirit.   Amen.

14th Sunday after Pentecost (Trinity 13)
THE FAMILY

231 Lord of the universe, we make our own rules because we cannot keep your laws; make us a new people, fit for a new heaven and a new earth, that we may live in harmony with all creation and with our God.   Amen.

232 Lord of life and love, who would not be shrouded in convention and hidden from the young, help us to see you as you are and to come, old and young, into your kingdom together, one in your resurrection and one in your love.   Amen.

15th Sunday after Pentecost (Trinity 14)
THOSE IN AUTHORITY

233 Holy Spirit of God, when our love for our neighbour conflicts with our duty to the state, make us like our Lord, who loved men and was killed by the state, who loved God and was raised from the dead.   Amen.

234 Lord and Saviour, keep us from following leaders whose lives lack love and whose ideals lack power; help us to be faithful to you, who died in love and rose in power to bring us to God.   Amen.

16th Sunday after Pentecost (Trinity 15)
THE NEIGHBOUR

235 Lord and Father, whose love flows through us like a river, sweep away the barriers which obstruct the flow, that we may give your love free passage through our lives to other people.   Amen.

236 Lord and Father, transplant in us a new heart of love, that we may see the hungry of the world lying at our door, and may offer not what we can spare but what they need, and be with them one family.   Amen.

17th Sunday after Pentecost (Trinity 16)
THE PROOF OF FAITH

237 Lord Jesus, your works were charged with the energy of God, recharge our faith; Lord Jesus, your works were left for us to finish, renew our strength; and bring the Father's glory into our lives and into the world.   Amen.

238 Lord Jesus, obedient to the Father in every detail of a crowded life, send us your orders and help us to obey, that we may know your truth, be the home of your Spirit and finish the work you have given us to do.   Amen.

18th Sunday after Pentecost (Trinity 17)
THE OFFERING OF LIFE

239 Lord, give us the courage to make amends for the hurt we cause to others and make us fit to live in your kingdom, where love alone inspires all thought and action, through Christ in whom we are forgiven.   Amen.

240 Lord Jesus, we are born unequal in many things, make us equal in this one thing: our determination to spend our lives for you and to use every faculty we have to spread the good news of your kingdom, until you come again.   Amen.

19th Sunday after Pentecost (Trinity 18)
THE LIFE OF FAITH

241 God of all being, you maintain all that exists, show us your
will and help us to obey, that in our present doing we may
find our eternal being and be your children now and for
ever.   Amen.

242 Father God, forgive us when we block the view of those who
look for your Son; make us what you would have us be, living
invitations into the joy of his presence.   Amen.

20th Sunday after Pentecost (Trinity 19)
ENDURANCE

243 Lord of glory, you set your face to finish the Father's work,
give us grace to finish the work we have begun, the spreading
of your Good News to all the world in our
generation.   Amen.

244 Lord of all power and goodness, when evil forces try to break
our minds, take our deepest motives and align them with
your will, that the bedrock of our being may be full
obedience.   Amen.

21st Sunday after Pentecost (Trinity 20)
THE CHRISTIAN HOPE

245 Lord, whose Son will come again in glory, send us hope; hope
for the future bringing present power; hope which looks
beyond all human help; hope in Christ, our present Saviour
and our future Judge.   Amen.

246 Lord God, faithful for ever, keep us faithful to you a day at a
time; teach us to pray today and to live in your presence

today, that at the end of time we may see your Son come again in glory.   Amen.

22nd Sunday after Pentecost (Trinity 21)
THE TWO WAYS

247 Lord, take our scattered thoughts and feelings and align them with your will; that the confinement of the narrow way may be our freedom and our delight and we may live now in the largeness of eternal life.   Amen.

248 Lord God, you have made us able to tell good from evil; give us grace always to follow the good, for the sake of our Lord who did your will at the cost of his life and made us free to follow him.   Amen.

Last Sunday after Pentecost
CITIZENS OF HEAVEN

249 Lord and Father, fill us with such love for your Son that our greatest need is to ask for his will to be done and our greatest reward the joy and peace of his presence.   Amen.

250 Lord, you prayed in Galilee, Gethsemane and on the cross; help us into the presence of the Father and teach us to pray, that we may know and love and obey our living God and see his kingdom come on earth.   Amen.

HARVEST

251 Creator God, we thank you for your promise that while the earth endures seed time and harvest, summer and winter, day and night, shall not fail. We thank you for the reliability of this good earth, for the variety of the seasons and for all the

unity and contrasts of creation. We thank you for this world's agenda for the labours of men and for permitting us to be partners to the earth's activity. We thank you that we can nourish the miracle of life upon the miracle of harvest and we praise you for the dignity of sharing in the work of your almighty hands, O God our Father, blessed for ever.   Amen.

252 We thank you, Lord, for the beauty and diversity of the world which you have made to be the mother of mankind. We thank you for making its hospitality to man endless in interest, loveliness, diversity and utility. Teach us by your creation to know more of you, our Creator, and, rejoicing in you, to be as generous to others as you are to us; through Jesus Christ our Lord.   Amen.

253 Creator God, you have provided man with everything he needs for life and health. Grant that the resources of the earth may not be hoarded by the selfish or squandered by the foolish, but that all may share your gifts, through our Lord Jesus Christ.   Amen.

Farm Workers

254 We thank you, Lord, for our companions who, through work in field and farm, earn their livelihood by providing us with ours. Give them good working conditions, happy relations with the rest of the community, a fair reward for their labours and the satisfaction which can come from seeing the works of the Lord in the labour of their hands; through Jesus Christ our Lord.   Amen.

Agricultural Research

255 Eternal Father, your mind devised the mightiness of seeds: we ask you to bless all who seek to understand the mysteries of creation. Make their thoughts to be partners of your own and grant that from the union of divine wisdom and human endeavour the resources of creation may be released to meet

the needs of mankind, through Jesus Christ our
Lord.　Amen.

256 Creator God, you made man and set him to tend the earth,
help us not to forget the sources of our physical life and may
the world of technology and trade never blind us to the
simple equation of soil and toil which gives us bread, through
Jesus Christ our Lord.　Amen.

257 Lord Jesus Christ, who came to earth that we might have life,
and have it abundantly: give us the capacity always to enjoy
your gifts to us and especially the gift of life itself, that
through these gifts we may learn to enjoy the supreme gift of
eternal life, shared forever with you and the Father and the
Holy Spirit, world without end.　Amen.

258 God our Father, we thank you for the world and for all your
gifts to us; for the sky above, for the earth beneath our feet,
for the wonderful process which provides our food. We thank
you for our crops and for the skills and techniques needed to
grow and share them properly. Help us to use your gifts in
the spirit of the Giver, through Jesus Christ our
Lord.　Amen.

259 We thank you, God, for the harvest of all good things: for
making plants that grow in the earth; for giving men
strength to work; for supplying the food we have each day.
Teach us to use your gifts fairly and generously and to
remember that you gave them to us: we ask it through Jesus
Christ our Lord.　Amen.

A Countryman's Litany at Harvest

260 Surrounded by the beauty of flowers and the fruits of harvest,
let us thank God for the loveliness of creation. Let us thank
him for the joy and wonder that the sight of beauty brings.
And let us pray for those who are blind or whose sight is
fading, that God will enrich them with the vision of beauty.
　　Lord in your mercy: hear our prayer.

We thank God for gardens in which we grow flowers, fruit
and vegetables and remember those who have no gardens to
grow things in and few places where their children can play.
Let us pray for children who have never picked a flower from
their own garden and for youngsters who have never climbed
a tree. Let us pray, too, for parents facing each day the
frustrations of living in tall blocks of flats or filthy slums.

Lord in your mercy: hear our prayer.

The things we have brought to this church are part of our
plenty, but millions never have enough to eat. Let us ask
God's forgiveness for our indifference to the needs of others.
Let us ask God's forgiveness that we forget that much of the
wealth of this country was gained by exploiting others. Let us
pray that as a nation and as individuals we may take seriously
our responsibilities for those who are starving.

Lord in your mercy: hear our prayer.

As we thank God for the provision of our needs as
individuals, let us remember that God is concerned for us as a
community. Let us pray for our community life here, for
those in positions of authority; for those who have recently
moved here; for those who find it difficult to accept the
changes taking place.

Lord in your mercy: hear our prayer.

The beauty of harvest makes us think of God, but millions in
our land and throughout the world, do not know God's love
for them and have not responded to Christ's invitation to find
in him their rest. Let us pray for those who have never trusted
their lives to Christ. Let us pray for ourselves and our
representatives in the missionary societies as together we tell
people of the Lord Jesus Christ and his love for them.

Lord in your mercy: hear our prayer.

Today we have remembered to thank God for his goodness.
But this reminds us that often we forget to be thankful. Let us
pray that we may never be complacent about the good things
we enjoy.

Lord in your mercy: hear our prayer.

Children's Prayer at Harvest

261 As we see the gifts brought here to remind us of God's
kindness, let us give him thanks for the food we eat. For food
which grows in gardens: lettuces, beans, carrots and
tomatoes.
> *For these gifts: we thank you, God our Father.*

For fields of peas, potatoes, cabbages and sugar beet.
> *For these gifts: we thank you God our Father.*

For crops of wheat and the flour for making bread and cakes.
> *For these gifts: we thank you, God our Father.*

For apples and pears and plums grown in orchards.
> *For these gifts: we thank you, God our Father.*

For the harvest of the sea—fish and crabs and shrimps.
> *For these gifts: we thank you, God our Father.*

For food from other lands: bananas and oranges and fruit in
tins.
> *For these gifts: we thank you, God our Father.*

For the work of farmers, fishermen, shopkeepers and all who
provide the things we need.
> *For these gifts: we thank you, God our Father.*

We thank you, God our Father, for your love in giving so
much to us. Help us to remember that your gifts are meant
for everyone. Help us to find ways of sharing with those who
are poor or hungry: for your love's sake.   Amen.

PRAYERS FOR ANIMALS

262 God our Father, you have given us animals to share with us
our life on earth: help us to show our gratitude to you by
treating them humanely and grant that men may give the
animals in their charge happy and contented lives, in return
for the food and service which they provide for us. We ask
this through Jesus Christ our Lord.   Amen.

263 Lord God, you have given us dominion over the animals and
we must one day give account of our stewardship; inspire us
with true reverence for your creation. Guide into the way of

kindness all who have the care of animals and bless all those who work to prevent or relieve suffering among them, through Jesus Christ our Lord.   Amen.

264 Father in heaven, your tender mercies are over all your work: send your blessing on those who care for sick and suffering animals and hasten the day when the whole of the animal creation shall be delivered from the bondage of cruelty and fear; through Jesus Christ our Lord.   Amen.

265 Blessed Lord, Father of compassion, you love all things great and small, and by your care the foxes have holes and the birds of the air have nests: bless all your creatures abundantly. Feed them and shelter them. Shield them from terror and torment and heal their wounds, through Jesus Christ our Lord.   Amen.

266 Lord, teach us to accept with gratitude and delight the beauty and wonder of the animal creation. You made them, they are yours and you have given them into our hands. Through greed, through selfishness, through curiosity, we woefully misuse them. Change the hearts of all men that these things shall not be.

Save us from exacting from them too high a price in pain in order to prolong our lives a little. In laboratory and farm, O Lord, may we be merciful to the helpless, through Jesus Christ our Lord.   Amen.

ONE WORLD WEEK

267 We thank you, Lord, for weaving into one great web the life of every age and every land. We thank you that this makes each moment of time a starting point for work of endless influence. Help us to accept the fact that our starting place is here and now; and may the world-wide web feel the pressure of our prayers today; through him who is the Beginner and the Completer of our faith, Jesus Christ our Lord.   Amen.

268 Lord, we pray for our fellow men on earth. Make us all to be more aware of our interdependence. Help us to know our need to care for the earth which sustains our life. Save governments and all who organize for power from destroying man or nature in pursuit of sectional interests. Educate the appetites and assumptions of ordinary people. Give generosity to the strong and prepare the weak for strength, that power may be used with restraint, by rich and poor alike. So may global repentance give to mankind a new mind, through Jesus Christ our Lord. Amen.

269 O God, you have measured us against this hour and the challenge is in simple, basic things which govern the way we think and live and pray. The needs are so vast and we are so weak that we despair of being effective servants. So we thank you for the knowledge that the work is Christ's and that we are members of his great body. Help us to be at one with the Lord of creation in the work of recreation. Help us to begin to join you in your work. Help us to begin here. Help us to begin now; through Jesus Christ our Lord. Amen.

270 Grant to each nation, O Lord, the greatness of spirit which does not need to feed upon the image of its greatness, but feeds instead upon the truth of God and the goal of international good. So may nations, like men, find greatness in service and as peacemakers be blessed as children of God: through Jesus Christ our Lord. Amen.

271 Grant to all nations, O Lord, a new vision of the family of man and the fatherhood of God. Grant us all to discern the true role of nationhood in the life of mankind. Grant that variety of tradition, rightly preserved and rightly shared, may help create true commonwealth. So may mankind reflect the glory of creation and the splendour of your kingdom, through Jesus Christ our Lord. Amen.

272 Heavenly Father, guide scientists and industrialists as together they create new industries. Give governments at every level wisdom and vision to make practical provisions for

necessary change. And lead all nations into ways which will
employ the powers of mankind for the good of all, through
Jesus Christ our Lord.   Amen.

Intercessions for use at the Eucharist

273 (The following may be used as supplements within the
pattern of the intercessions at the Eucharist, or they may be
used as a series of separate prayers.)

For the church

We pray for all who bring help to stricken people; we pray
that we may be one with them. Grant that we and every
member of your church may be good stewards of the earth,
good stewards of the gospel and a sign of unity in a divided
world. By personal life-style and genuine community make
us, O Lord, to be credible Christians.

For the world and our nation

Grant, O Lord, that the leaders of rich countries and poor
countries may all alike be given a vision of your purpose for
men and nations, to bring all things into unity in Christ:
unite their endeavours in wealth and poverty to make strong
the poor and give true wealth to the rich, that all mankind
may find a genuinely human existence.

For the local community

Save us from requiring of leaders virtues we do not practise
ourselves; may the good we seek in the international
community first be practised in our own locality by ourselves.
Help us to a new awareness that the whole world begins with
our neighbour and our next of kin.

For the sick

We pray for each individual member of the multitudes born
into situations which create disease and death; for those
without family, food or medical help; for all who are stricken
by the corporate sin of all mankind.

The passing generations

We remember, Father, the millions made in your own image but born into our world only to be rejected by it, to die without knowing strength, health or joy: may mankind not forget them, but by the power of the cross may what is past help shape a better future until you bring all things into unity in Christ.

REMEMBRANCE SUNDAY

Father Forgive

274 'All have sinned and come short of the glory of God' (Romans 3:23 AV).

The hatred which divides nation from nation, race from race, class from class,
Father forgive.
The covetous desires of men and nations to possess what is not their own,
Father forgive.
The greed which exploits the labours of men and lays waste the earth,
Father forgive.
Our envy of the welfare and happiness of others,
Father forgive.
Our indifference to the plight of the homeless and the refugee,
Father forgive.
The lust which uses for ignoble ends the bodies of men and women,
Father forgive,
'Be kind to one another, tenderhearted, forgiving one another, as God in Christ forgave you' (Ephesians 4:32 RSV).

An Act of Resolve

275 It is our resolve to save succeeding generations from the
scourge of war which many times in this century has brought
untold sorrow to mankind.
Lord help us.
It is our resolve to reaffirm our faith in fundamental human
rights, in the dignity and worth of every human person, in
the equal rights of men and women and of nations large and
small.
Lord help us.
It is our resolve to establish conditions under which justice,
and respect for the obligations arising from treaties and other
sources of international law, can be maintained, and to
promote social progress and better standards of life in larger
freedom.
Lord help us.
And for these ends it is our resolve to practise tolerance and
live together in peace with one another as good neighbours.
Lord help us.
It is our resolve to unite our strength to maintain
international peace and security and to ensure that armed
force shall not be used save in the common interest.
Lord help us.
It is our resolve to employ international machinery for the
promotion of the economic and social advancement of all
peoples.
Lord help us.

An Act of Remembrance

276 Father, we remember before you the needs of those who suffer
because of war. We know you need no reminder of their
trouble: your compassion is the same whether we remember
them or not. It is we who need to remember. We remember
them before you now. We remember them because you are
their father as well as ours.
   (Silence)
We thank you, Father, for reminding us that remembrance is

not enough; for reminding us that helping them is the
Christian family's business. We remember them so that you
may guide us into the best way of helping them.
(Silence)
Save us, Father, from the blasphemy of making intercession
merely an act of church routine. May formal worship not
become meaningless ritual. Show us what we must do. Help
us to do it.
(Silence)
Let us not plead poverty of time or money or talent, for we can
always find time to do what we want to do; we can always find
money to spend on what we really desire; we can always find
jobs within our powers. Help us to help the helpless. Turn
our prayer into action. And give our action good success;
through Jesus Christ our Lord. Amen.

277 O Saviour Christ, in you there is neither Jew nor Greek, East
nor West, black nor white: we pray for all in every nation who
suffer because of human strife, especially for those least able
to receive human help; those whose hearts are still bitter;
those whom we remember today. We pray that through your
ministry of love and life their wounds of body and spirit may
be healed and that in you men may find peace with God and
peace with one another; for your truth and mercy's
sake. Amen.

278 O Father of mercies and God of all comfort, ~~your Son
ministered to those in need:~~ remember for good all who suffer
through the wars of men and nations by loss of home or
faculties, by loss of friends and loved ones, by loss of
happiness, security or freedom. Look upon our world, still
torn apart by violence and fighting, and grant success to those
who work for peace: through him who reconciled men with
God, and men with men, the Lord Jesus Christ. Amen.

279 O God, whose Son Jesus Christ lived and worked in this
world, and knew its hatred and its war, its diseases and its
sin, please help those who have to find a way out of this
deadlock to progress; a way out of division to harmony; a way

out of selfishness to co-operation; a way out of death to life.
Grant them wisdom, restraint and a desire for fair and just
dealing.

Channel the strong desire for peace among many people
into useful and constructive ways of peace making and bring
your own rule of peace among the men you have created; for
the sake of Jesus Christ our Lord.   Amen.

280 O God of power and love, look in mercy upon our war-torn
world, which is still your world. You have made it; in it you
delight to work; you have redeemed its people. Grant
reconciliation, we pray, between man and man, nation and
nation, through the power of that great peace made by Jesus
your Son. May your servants not be troubled by wars and
rumours of wars, but rather look up because their redemption
draws near. And when our King returns, may he find many
waiting for him and fighting with his weapons alone: we ask
this in the King's name, Jesus Christ your Son, our
Lord.   Amen.

281 We continue to pray, O Lord, for the peace of the world.
Help us to see that there can be no peace among nations
unless there is peace among men and no peace among men
until men have made their peace with you. We claim the
peace which comes from faith in Jesus Christ, that having
peace in our hearts we may be at peace with our neighbours
and that peace between man and man may finally grow into
peace between nation and nation. We ask this in the name of
the Prince of peace, our Lord Jesus Christ.   Amen.

282 O God, we pray that wars may come to an end, and that
domination of one country over another, one class over
another, one colour over another, may soon become a thing of
the past; through Jesus Christ our Lord.   Amen.

283 O God of peace, we confess that wars and strife are all of
mankind's making. Forgive the blasphemy which lays the
blame on you. And give us grace to see that when we blame
ourselves there is a light in our darkness. Then, O God, give

us strength to order our affairs in the power of that light and so to love and speak the truth in love, that others may look with us to you and in you find the way, the truth and the life for all mankind, through Jesus Christ our Lord.   Amen.

284   Almighty God, who made all men to be of one blood, look in mercy on the nations which now confront each other in anger, fear and pride. Enable their leaders to see in their true perspective those things which divide them, and to see in their true importance those things which may unite. And in your grace and mercy, Lord, inspire all men everywhere to cease from war and to fight instead for those things which you have shown us to be right in Jesus Christ, for his name's sake.   Amen.

285   Have mercy, Lord, on all who seek to solve their nation's problems by force of arms; those who seek to strengthen their national economy by promoting international strife; those who divert a nation's mind from corruption at home by talk of enmity abroad; those who see young men at arms as pawns upon a gaming board; and all who are eager through warfare to barter with others in flesh and blood. Upon these and all who hate their brother, have mercy, Lord, we pray and turn their hearts, through Jesus Christ our Lord.   Amen.

Soldiers

286   Father, we pray for all young soldiers caught up in the conflict and horror of war. May fear and confusion not lead them to cruelty. May they show compassion wherever possible. Enable them to fulfil their duty without hatred so that their souls may not be scarred by the passions let loose in war; through Jesus Christ our Lord.   Amen.

287   We thank you, Lord, for the journalists and cameramen who risk their lives to rob warfare of its glamour. May we take to heart their portrait of men's pain and never think of war except in terms of sorrow; through Jesus Christ our Lord.   Amen.

288 O Lord Jesus Christ, Prince of peace, break down the barriers
which separate men from each other and from God. Teach
Christians to love each other across the walls of colour, class
and creed. Forgive us, too, the excuses we make for our own
prejudice and lead us captive in your cause of peace on earth,
goodwill to men, for your name's sake.   Amen.

**Five Prayers Offered at the Falklands Service in St Paul's
Cathedral, 1982.**

289 God our Father, we praise you for the gospel of
reconciliation. We thank you for the work of the Holy Spirit
drawing the scattered flock of Christ into a deeper unity. May
this be a sign of hope to our divided world. Enable us, who
bear your name, to be instruments of your peace and ever to
believe that the peace for which we pray is possible; through
Jesus Christ our Lord.   Amen.

290 God of all nations, we thank you for the concern for peace
which grows in the hearts and minds of ordinary people the
world over. Use that concern to create the structures of peace
and a new atmosphere of cooperation. Help us to identify the
common enemies of all mankind and to work together for the
eradication of poverty, hunger and disease. Give us the will
to build defences against these instead of against each other;
for the sake of Jesus Christ our Saviour.   Amen.

291 Eternal God, as the rainbow spans the heavens when the
clouds are dark, so our strifes and enmities stand under the
judgement of your over-arching love and righteousness. We
thank you for those who were in former times our enemies,
but are now our friends. Grant that the work of reconciliation
may now bring lasting peace where there has been strife and
justice and security for all the peoples of the earth, for Jesus
Christ's sake.   Amen.

292 O Christ, our Master and Redeemer, you were wounded for
the salvation of all mankind, your body broken for the peace
of the world. Hear us, therefore, as we now commend to your

loving care all who have been wounded in body, mind or spirit in recent conflict: the blind, the maimed, the disabled, the mentally distraught, all for whom life will never now be the same. Grant them healing of body and mind, strengthening of spirit and confidence and, whatever the future holds for them, the encouragement of good companionship and of understanding love, for your dear sake. Amen.

293 Lord our God, you guide your creation with fatherly care. Your will is to gather all peoples as one family in yourself. Banish violence from our midst and wipe away our tears, so that we may not only be called your sons and daughters, but live as true brothers and sisters in Christ your Son. Amen.

ALL SAINTS DAY

294 Eternal God, help us always to remember the great unseen cloud of witnesses round about us. When in danger, give us their courage and when in difficulty, their perseverance; so that we too may be faithful until we rejoice with all the saints in your eternal kingdom, through Jesus Christ our Lord. Amen.

295 We thank you, O God, for the example of the saints. Help us to follow in their footsteps with courage and with hope, so that your work on earth may be faithfully continued and your holy name be praised until the end of the world, through Jesus Christ our Lord. Amen.

296 Almighty God, we praise your holy name for all the saints throughout the ages who have kept the lamp of faith burning brightly. Grant that we who are following in their steps may keep that light shining, that the darkness of this world may be lit by him who is the light of the world, even your Son our Saviour, Jesus Christ. Amen.

NEW YEAR

For a Watch Night Service

297 Look upon us tonight, Lord, as we pray to you with our tiny resolutions and enormous fears, our tiny achievements and enormous failings, our tiny vision and enormous tasks. Be with those who are very conscious of the vanity and frustration of this world and show them that Christ makes all things new. Be with those also who do not feel this frustration: be with the self-satisfied, the rich, the proud and the powerful, that they may see in Christ a much more excellent way.

Look upon our homes and families and dear ones; those from whom we are separated, those for whom we are anxious, those with whom we have quarrelled. Bring into every human relationship the unity and healing and strength of your Son.

Look upon our church in all its needs. Come among us in refreshing and reviving power in this coming year.

Look upon our world with all its waste and war and sorrow and all its joys as well; and make your believing people more effective in serving it, in bringing it light and sharing with it the fragrance of Christ.

All these things we ask for the honour of his name.   Amen.

298 Lord of time and new beginnings, give us good judgement to know what new things to do for you this year and grant us the inner strength to finish each job we begin; so may we fully know the joy of doing your will; so may your kingdom come on earth; through Jesus Christ our Lord.   Amen.

299 Help us, O Lord, to enter this new year as your people of old entered their promised land: give us, like them, a sense of vocation; give us, like them, the promise of your presence: so may this year, in all its possibilities for good and ill, be lived with power, in fellowship with you, in harmony of spirit and for the good of all mankind: through Jesus Christ our Lord.   Amen.

300 Grant Lord, that as the years change we may find rest in your
eternal changelessness. May we go forward into this year with
courage, sure in the faith that while life changes around us,
you are always the same, guiding us with your wisdom and
protecting us with your love. So may the peace which passes
understanding keep our hearts and minds in Christ Jesus and
your blessing be upon all nations and upon all whom we love,
in the name of the Father and of the Son and of the Holy
Spirit.   Amen.

301 All through this year, O Father, help me to know Christ
better, and to make him better known, by yielding my will
to the lordship of Christ and my life to the service of others,
for Jesus Christ's sake.   Amen.

302 'Jesus said, "My command is this: Love each other as I have
loved you. Greater love has no-one than this, that one lay
down his life for his friends"' (John 15:12–13).
   Lord Jesus, forgive us. We have not kept your
commandment. We have hardly started to keep it. We are so
far away from laying down our lives for our friends that we
cannot even lay down our prejudices, our likes and dislikes;
our ways of doing things; our needs and comforts.
   Lord Jesus, forgive us. We talk of changing society and we
cannot even change our own bad habits, or straighten out the
bends we make in the road to avoid treading on old, forgotten
hurts.
   Lord Jesus, you laid down your life for us so that we could
change.
   Make us new, Lord. Fill us with your love. Open us to love
each other. And as citizens of your city, where the tree of life
grows, whose leaves are for the healing of the nations, make
us to be channels of your peace and healing in our
world.   Amen.

PART 2

Prayers for the World and the Church

THE QUEEN, RULERS AND GOVERNORS

303 Grant, O Lord, to Her Majesty the Queen simple faith to walk in the way set before her; patience and courage to bear the burden laid upon her; humility to know that her sovereignty is but lent by you; and the sure hope of life with you for ever, to whom belongs all dignity and greatness, all majesty and power, in both this world and that which is to come. Amen.

304 Lord God almighty, King of creation, bless our Queen and all in authority under her. May godliness be their goal; may sanctity be their strength; may peace on earth be the fruit of their labours; and joy in heaven their eternal gift, through Jesus Christ our Lord. Amen.

305 Almighty God, our heavenly Father, we pray for our Queen and the Royal Family, the Members of Parliament and all in authority: that they may govern our country with wisdom and understanding and for the good of your church and people, through Jesus Christ our Lord. Amen.

306 Almighty God, the Scriptures command us to pray for all in authority. We recognize that all ultimate authority is yours and leaders derive their power to rule from you.
   Guide Her Majesty the Queen and all her ministers and all the rulers of the world. Help them to make decisions which are good; to make laws which are just; and to make policies

which uphold human dignity, and are in accord with the truths found in holy Scripture.   Amen.

307 We thank you, heavenly Father, for the ways in which you have led this nation over the centuries: for the way you have enabled us to devise and adapt a way of government which makes evolution possible and revolution pointless.

We thank you for the role which has been achieved by the monarchy and for a head of state who is above party loyalties and independent of the changes these bring.

We thank you for the ways in which the Queen has exercised in her own life and character the virtues which are necessary to a healthy national life.

We pray that you will bless her in this year and in all those which are to come, granting her public fortitude and private happiness and the protection of your fatherly care; through Jesus Christ our Lord.   Amen.

308 Grant, Lord, to all the leaders of men the wisdom to seek what is right and the goodness to do it; may learning, education and politics all be directed to good ends; and may godliness among men lead to peace among nations; through Jesus Christ our Lord.   Amen.

THE NATION

309 God bless our land; God guide our rulers; God resolve our differences; God revive our churches; God forgive our selfishness; God protect our homes; God strengthen our faith; through Jesus Christ our Lord.   Amen.

310 Heavenly Father, help us to become masters of ourselves that we may become servants of others; help us to serve God and honour the Queen; help us to put Christ first, others second, and ourselves last, for Jesus Christ's sake.   Amen.

311 Father in heaven, whose will it is that all should worship you in the fellowship of the church and serve you in the life of the

world, send down upon our nation a true spirit of repentance
for the sinfulness which passes as broadmindedness, the
apathy which calls itself tolerance, the materialism which
glories in its prosperity and grasps for more. And with this
sorrow, O Lord God, let faith and obedience go hand in hand,
that men's lives may be transformed, that integrity and
godliness may characterize our people, to your praise and
honour; through Jesus Christ our Lord.   Amen.

312 Grant to our nation, O Lord, a knowledge of that which is
good by which to measure that which is doubtful. Help those
who influence public opinion never to presume that people
are wiser or better than their forebears, nor more able than
they to cope with the consequences of sin. And raise up we
pray a new knowledge of Christ in the hearts and minds of all
who work in the creative arts, for the sake of Jesus Christ our
Lord.   Amen.

313 O mighty God, the source of all goodness, we ask you to bless
those who are in positions of power and authority in this
country. Bless the Queen and all the Royal Family, the Prime
Minister, the Cabinet and all Members of Parliament. Enrich
them with your grace and fill them with your Holy Spirit,
that we may be governed with wisdom and godliness by
Christian men and women, through Jesus Christ our
Lord.   Amen.

Civil Strife

314 Great God of peace, be present where there is civil strife;
where neighbour rises up against neighbour, where familiar
streets become battlefields and familiar people become the
casualties. Change the hearts of all those who think that their
cause is more important than another man's right to live;
change the policies of those on either side which create,
condone or extend the conflict; and by the power of the cross
help all who sin to repent, and all who have been sinned
against to forgive, that peace may come, through Jesus Christ
our Lord.   Amen.

315 Dear God, you have decreed that righteousness alone shall make a nation great, we beseech you so to move the hearts and wills of our leaders and people that in righteousness we may be led and in righteousness may gladly follow; for the honour of your name, through Jesus Christ our Lord.   Amen.

316 From you alone, O Lord, comes love and trust; in you alone, O Lord, can men and nations find their peace. Send into the hearts of all men everywhere the transforming power of your Spirit, so that with new heart and purpose we may seek first your service and the service of one another and in so doing discover the peace which passes understanding, through Jesus Christ our Lord.   Amen.

THE CHURCH

317 Lord of the church, enable your people to be the church: a redeemed people; a holy people; a united people; a missionary people; and in all things a people gladly submissive to the truth as it comes to us in Jesus, in whose name we pray.   Amen.

318 Almighty God, you have made us members of Christ in a local congregation. Open our eyes to see truth clearly through the ministry of the word of God. Open our hearts to love Christ dearly, through the ministry of the sacraments. Open our imaginations widely through the ministry of pastoral care. May our congregation reach upwards to your throne in worship and adoration; inwards to one another in understanding and fellowship; and outwards to the world in evangelism and social compassion.

   Make us like a city set upon a hill whose light cannot be darkened, so that men and women may find Christ as the Light of the world, and his church as the family of the redeemed, and eternal life as the gift of God, through Jesus Christ our Lord.   Amen.

319 We thank you, Lord, for raising up in every land people of all cultures to call you Father and be our brothers. Help us to learn from one another more of your Fatherhood, more of our brotherhood, more of our faith, more of ourselves: that we may glorify you in the church and in Christ Jesus, now and forever.   Amen.

320 Thank you, God, for the courage and the faith of all those who from the time of the apostles preached the gospel of the living Christ: those who were strong in the face of persecution; those who brought the good news to this land of ours; and those who in recent years have gone out to teach and preach in the name of Christ their Lord.

  Be with your church in every land. Strengthen her where she is weak, encourage her where she is failing; give her humility where she is proud and self-confident; and where day by day she is seeking to show others the joy of your kingdom, deepen her faith in her risen Lord.

  Help us to realize that we are part of your great church universal and that together with all your children we can worship and adore, through Jesus Christ our Lord.   Amen.

321 O heavenly Father, the same yesterday, today and forever, pour your blessing upon the ministers and laymen of your church, in this country and in all lands. May we grasp your majesty and might; may we be filled with your Holy Spirit, that the church today, like the early church, may preach and live the gospel of Christ in eagerness, power and love. Grant this, O Lord, that your name may be honoured before the world.   Amen.

322 O merciful God, we commit to you all those who make up your church in all the world. Teach us, whom you have justified, to live by faith; bear us by your grace through all troubles; and bring us at last to the glory of your eternal kingdom; for the honour of our Saviour and Mediator, Jesus Christ.   Amen.

323 We are ashamed, O God, for our carelessness in worship: for wandering minds and thoughtless prayer. We are ashamed that words of praise come so swiftly to our lips but so slowly to our hearts. We are ashamed that we bear the name of Jesus but act as if he were a stranger.

Forgive us for our jealousies in the church and for the irritations which so easily win the day. Forgive us for the times when we can see plainly what needs to be done and complain that others do not do it.

Give us, O Lord, a vision of our church among people who do not know Christ as Lord and give to us a deepened faith, an understanding love, a ready wit, and the Holy Spirit's uncommon sense. May we so live and preach that our neighbours want to know the source of the joy we have, through Jesus Christ our Lord.   Amen.

Reshaping the Church

324 Guide and direct, O Lord, the minds of all who work for the reshaping of our church. Restore our faith and vision. Renew our energies and love. Revive your people to new life and power. So may we live and speak for Christ before the world he came to save; for his name's sake.   Amen.

325 As patterns of Christian ministry change to meet the changing life of city, town and countryside, give wisdom, Lord, to those whose vision leads the way. May they help others to believe, to pray, to love, to serve: that your holy church may be at one with that which was and that which is to come, through Jesus Christ our Lord.   Amen.

For Chairmen of Committees

326 Give to those who serve as chairmen of committees, Lord, a broad vision, a patient spirit, an understanding heart and a practical turn of mind. Give them wisdom to handle people and procedures aright and guide them to a true sense of priorities. Grant that by skill and service they may enable

energy to be released in tasks which have been rightly discerned, through Jesus Christ our Lord.   Amen.

For a Balanced Commitment

327 Grant, O Lord, a right balance of your powers in us, that in loving you singly we may not neglect the needs of man and that in serving mankind wholeheartedly we may not forget the joys of the world to come. Give us the gifts of faith and hope and love in perfect measure, that we may look upwards, look outwards and look onwards, with equal eagerness, through Jesus Christ our Lord.   Amen.

328 We thank you, Father, for your gift of perfect love, for Jesus Christ. We thank you for all who have accepted your gift and in whom the light shines. For those who seek to improve the plight of the homeless and the badly housed; for the young people sharing their learning and energy freely through voluntary service at home and abroad; for all organizations helping to relieve suffering and distress in stricken lands; for missionaries living out your message in the midst of ignorance, fear and disease; for all those who freely give time and energy and money to bring comfort, hope and help to someone who needs it. Your light shines in the darkness and the darkness has not overcome it. We thank you, Father, for this, through Jesus Christ our Lord.   Amen.

A Parish Awaiting a New Minister

329 Lord, call to this your church and ours a true shepherd, a man of God, a minister of Christ. Make us, with him, a church joyful in worship, united in witness, working, caring, praising, loving: to the glory of your name; through Jesus Christ our Lord.   Amen.

Theologians

330 Eternal God, you are the beginning and the ending of our faith: teach us how to understand unchanging truth in

changing times; bless all those who think new thoughts for love of Christ; help us as we share those thoughts in the fellowship of the church; and grant to us all a deepening knowledge of eternal truth; through Jesus Christ our Lord. Amen.

Annual Meetings and Parochial Church Councils

331 God of time and new beginnings, bless the annual meeting of this church (or society, organization etc.). May it take its character from your presence. Give us the spirit of praise for your blessings, and penitence for our failures. Help us so to learn from the past as to gain vision for the future. So may the present moment be one of gratitude, dedication and hope, for the glory of your name. Amen.

332 O Holy Spirit of God, we ask for your presence and guidance at the meeting of the Church Council (this week). May each member exercise his or her responsibilities wisely and prayerfully and may the decisions of the Council be in accordance with your will and for the extension of Christ's kingdom in this parish, for his name's sake. Amen.

333 Heavenly Father, send your Holy Spirit to guide all members of church councils. May all who are called to this work be committed to serving and pleasing you, so that the work of the church in the world may be helped forward and not hindered, through Jesus Christ our Lord. Amen.

334 Lord, guide us as we meet together that we may think calmly and carefully, decide wisely and well, in order that everything may be done in accordance with your will. Help us to make your concerns our concerns, so that through us you may be able to carry on your work here on earth, for Jesus Christ's sake. Amen.

For an Increase in Congregation

335 Heavenly Father, we continue to pray that you will multiply

the number of worshippers in your church of. . .; that we may be drawn together purely by love of yourself and for your glory; that your love may become the mainspring of our lives, so that we may show love to each other and to those around us. Change us into your likeness, through the mighty love of your Son, Jesus Christ our Lord.   Amen.

Building a New Church

336 Almighty Father, we thank you for setting us the task of building a new church in this parish, a church where generations yet unborn shall worship you; look graciously upon our efforts, we beseech you. Inspire us by your Spirit, that we may not become despondent, but may have faith to match all difficulties, believing that in your strength we may soon lay its foundations with joy and build its walls in hope. We ask this through our Lord and Saviour Jesus Christ.   Amen.

The Dedication of Churches and Patronal Festivals

337 Almighty God, forever present in creation, eternally greater than all that is in it, have mercy on us who have built this church for your praise. Save us from idolatry. As we learn to meet you here may we learn to meet you everywhere. And may our reverence for this place teach us how to view the whole creation, through Jesus Christ our Lord.   Amen.

Architects

338 Almighty God, architect of the universe, bless your servants who design cathedrals, churches and chapels for your praise. May their work express the majesty of your being, the integrity of your creation, the pattern of your speech, the manner of your coming, the nature of your abiding, the spirit of our response, the shape of our community, the goal of our discipleship; for your most worthy praise.   Amen.

Ancient Churches

339 We thank you, Lord, for the rich heritage of ancient churches in this land: for the gospel which they silently proclaim and the living history to which they bear witness. Help us to care for them aright, to adapt them wisely to their continuing task and to preserve the spirit of those who built them: that generations yet unborn may find in them the rock from which they have been hewn and themselves be born again as living stones in the church of God eternal, through Jesus Christ our Lord.   Amen.

340 Bless those, O Lord, who make their churches centres of hospitality for those who visit them on weekdays; those who welcome visitors of every kind; those who open their doors to the lonely and the sad, and to seekers after solace, meaning, inspiration or fellowship. Give to members of those churches the spirit of love and wisdom, that they may perceive aright the need for speech or silence. As doorkeepers of the house of the Lord make them a blessing, and give them a blessing, through Jesus Christ our Lord.   Amen.

PRAYERS FOR UNITY

At an Ecumenical Meeting

341 Pope John Paul's Canterbury prayer

O Christ, may all that is part of today's encounter be born of the Spirit of truth and be made fruitful through love.
    Behold before us: the past and the future.
    Behold before us: the desires of so many hearts.
    You, who are the Lord of history and the Lord of human hearts, be with us. Christ Jesus, eternal Son of God, be with us.   Amen.
(Prayed by Pope John Paul II in Canterbury Cathedral 29th June 1982)

342 Forgive us the sins of disunity, Lord; pride and jealousy and narrow-mindedness. Forgive us the sins of unity: lack of imagination, apathy and indifference. Make us one in genuine love and mutual trust. Make us many in gifts and talents and vision. Amen.

Litanies for Unity

343 Let us thank God that because man is made in his image it is possible for men to be united. Let us thank him for the special unity which those who are new creatures in Christ can enjoy. Let us ask God to forgive the sin that has destroyed the unity he meant mankind to have.
Lord in mercy: hear our prayer.
Let us thank God for the growth in understanding between Christians of different outlooks and traditions. Let us thank him for the growth in unity of our local churches. Let us pray that we may grow together in truth and love.
Lord in mercy: hear our prayer.
Let us pray that we may learn from Christians of other traditions. Let us pray that they may learn from us. May they and we remember that Jesus prayed for us to be sanctified in truth before he prayed for us to be one. Therefore let us pray that we might seek unity through the truth.
Lord in mercy: hear our prayer.
Let us pray for our own church, that we and all its members may be filled with the spirit of faith, hope and love and so attain to that unity which will cause people to acknowledge the truth of the gospel.
Lord in mercy: hear our prayer.
Let us pray for the community of which we are part. Let us pray for greater unity between its various sections, interests and age groups.
Lord in mercy: hear our prayer.
Let us pray for the unity of our country, for a greater understanding and sympathy between the young and those who are older; between employers and those employed; between immigrants and the host community; and between

the church and those who have rejected institutional
Christianity.
Lord in mercy: hear our prayer.
Finally, let us pray for the unity of the world, for
reconciliation, peace and compassion between rich and poor,
white and coloured, capitalist and communist and those
nations which have long been embattled.
Lord in mercy: hear our prayer.

344 Let us pray that all God's will for his church may be fulfilled
in it. And on this day let us pray particularly that all
ecumenical endeavour might be based firmly upon the word
of God, should have the aim of glorifying the Son of God,
should seek the power of the Spirit of God, should bear fruit
to the praise of God.
Lord in mercy: hear our prayer.
Let us pray that in all its present divisions the church may
preach the gospel with growing zeal, growing confidence,
growing power; so may the gospel itself unite us. And let us
pray that the unity thus given may itself commend and make
persuasive the gospel we proclaim.
Lord in mercy: hear our prayer.
Let us pray that we may be saved from worshipping any
tradition, no matter how excellent. Let us pray that we may
be saved from worshipping any hope, no matter how
glorious. Let us pray that we may be saved from these and all
forms of idolatry, that we may be set free to worship God, the
Father Almighty.
Lord in mercy: hear our prayer.
Let us pray for theologians, thinkers and planners, who are
now engaged in finding the way to outward expressions of
unity, that they may deal in godliness and in truth, and
exercise their judgement in wisdom and love.
Lord in mercy: hear our prayer.
Let us pray for all who negotiate any difficult and painful
matter, which may arise in practical schemes of union, that
they may never forget that they are not dealing with
institutions, but with people and the risen Christ.
Lord in mercy: hear our prayer.

Let us pray for every experiment designed to help us see the traditions of others through their own eyes.

Lord in mercy: hear our prayer.

Let us pray for ourselves in our worship today that our eyes may not be upon our differences but upon Christ: that we may look to him and be saved.

Lord in mercy: hear our prayer.

Let us pray for the churches of this parish (here they may be named): that each may be blessed by God the Holy Spirit and be brought to that fullness of life in which we stand together under the lordship of Christ.

Lord in mercy: hear our prayer.

Let us pray for the children of our churches that to them may be revealed the unfolding purposes of your will and the vision of the church as it shall be.

Lord in mercy: hear our prayer.

And let us pray for ourselves that we may be given a vision of the world in all its need and be so inspired by God that we may serve it with grace and power. May we so love the truth and live the truth and speak the truth that all men everywhere may find the truth, and being set free from sin find the glorious liberty of the children of God.

Lord in mercy: hear our prayer.

345 Let us kneel and offer ourselves to God that we may know how to take our share in his design for the world. Let us pray that we may put ourselves alongside our fellow men and see the Christian faith and life from their point of view.

Lord, hear our prayer;

that the church may be aware of the rapid rate of change both in the thought of men and in their social circumstances:

Lord, hear our prayer;

for the wisdom of the Holy Spirit in the large scale and complex problems of society and work today, which require corporate judgements and solutions:

Lord, hear our prayer;

that in the choices facing mankind today, in situations partly good and partly evil, we may be granted the insights of the

Holy Spirit and guided to make decisions which will forward your will:

> *Lord, hear our prayer;*

that you will grant to Christians working in big organizations the faith that they can share in some small way your active concern for the good ordering of men's lives and the supplying of their needs:

> *Lord, hear our prayer;*

that we may see in our daily work the opportunity for serving you by the truth of our insights, the honesty of our service and concern for our fellow workers:

> *Lord, hear our prayer;*

that you will bless those groups of Christians who are trying to discover how they may best exercise Christian vocation through their professions:

> *Lord, hear our prayer;*

that our local churches may no longer be seen as arks of safety but as power-houses of grace for the invading forces of your kingdom:

> *Lord, hear our prayer;*

that you will bless and guide all lay movements which seek to advance your kingdom in special spheres of work or in particular neighbourhoods:

> *Lord, hear our prayer;*

that you will guide our local churches to face the challenge of such movements, to learn from them and to offer understanding and grateful fellowship:

> *Lord, hear our prayer;*

that you will enable the clergy to bring the light of your truth to their people and the grace of the sacraments to their strengthening:

> *Lord, hear our prayer;*

The Christian Family Tree

346 'I am the vine, you are the branches. If a man remains in me and I in him, he will bear much fruit' (John 15:5).

Father, we thank you for the fact, and for the history of our great family tree, of which we too are branches. And we give thanks for all those who have brought forth good fruit:

those who have overcome every hardship in order to take knowledge of you to all parts of the world;

those who have dedicated their lives to social work;

those who have visited prisoners and given them hope;

those who have fought disease and ignorance;

those who have brought colour and music and beauty into our lives through the expression of their faith;

those who have suffered to keep God's word pure and clear and free from men's additions;

those who in their family life by teaching and example have given to their children the desire to belong to this tree. Father, we are glad that we too are able to be branches of this great tree of life and we pray that our lives may bring forth good fruit to the glory of your name.   Amen.

347 Lord Jesus Christ, in you we see the Father's love—the love he gives us in the Spirit—and in that love we pray for all Christians: that they may renew their hope in the power of your Father who loves the world and saves it; for all men: that in the hour and by the means you choose you will unite them to yourself in love and truth.

Lord, hear our prayer.

May the Holy Spirit carry to the Father our prayer for unity: keep us, O God, from growing accustomed to our divisions; save us from considering as normal that which is a scandal to the world and an offence against your love.

Unite us in love and in truth.

Deliver us, O Lord, from a spirit of narrowness, of bitterness, or of prejudice. Teach us to recognize the gifts of your grace in all those who call upon you with an honest heart.

Unite us in love and truth.

Deepen our faithfulness to your word. Do not allow us to be led astray by our own delusions or to walk in paths which are not of your choosing.

Unite us in love and truth.

By your power, O Lord, gather your scattered flock. May it be united in you so that the purpose of your love may be fulfilled

and the world may know you to be one with the Father and
the Holy Spirit, God blessed for ever.   Amen.

At an Ordination Retreat

348 Lord, you commanded storm and tumult saying, 'Peace, be
still': breathe stillness now to our expectant hearts. Help us
to rest upon your faithfulness, to receive the fullness of your
love and to be at peace within our selves as ministers whom
Christ has called; for his name's sake.   Amen.

349 Grant, Lord, to those now called to ministry and service:
increasing knowledge of the living God, confidence in the
gospel and the word of life, compassion for the lost and
needy; courage, endurance and unfailing love; for Jesus
Christ's sake.   Amen.

THE CHURCH'S MISSION

Missionary Meetings

350 Awaken every sense, O Lord, to your presence in our midst.
May our meeting together be a meeting with you, and, if it
is your will, make it as unforgettable for us as those meetings
with other disciples in Galilee long ago. Therefore, Lord,
bless those who speak in your name. Clothe yourself in their
thoughts, appear to us in their words. So that through the
mystery of preaching and in the ministry of hearing, we may
behold you in our midst; for your dear name's sake.   Amen.

351 Lord, look upon us, solitary grains of wheat unwilling to die
but bearing within ourselves all that you require to speak to
the world. Save us, Lord, from living for ourselves, abiding
alone, imprisoned by our fears, isolated by our ambitions,
deformed by our conceit. May the Spirit of Jesus move us to
follow him; may the power of the cross make us take it up;
give us the power and give us the will and give us the
understanding to lay down our life. So shall we be free from

ourselves, free to bear much fruit, through Jesus Christ our Lord.   Amen.

352 Almighty God teach us afresh the meaning of almightiness, that whatever evil assails us we may have a deep and steady confidence in your power to guide, deliver and overcome; through Jesus Christ our Lord.   Amen.

353 Almighty God, give to your church the mastery over every system of thought which in the name of truth assails the truth: teach us to out-think the wisdom of this world. By the cross of Jesus renew in us the knowledge that not even almightiness can win the hearts of men except through pain and grief. Teach us, Lord, and all the church militant, to know the conditions on which men receive your power and to fulfil them, through Jesus Christ our Lord.   Amen.

354 We thank you, Lord, for all those who have seen Jesus in their inner life and who have given their lives as grains of wheat to the soil of your good purposes. We thank you in particular for all who have done this in fellowship with us and (name of missionary society).

Grant that they may all, day by day, discover the almightiness of your grace. Grant to them, new every morning, the refreshing knowledge of your love, and awareness of the wider Christian family whose life is bound up in theirs and holy communion with the life of heaven which sustains us all.

Graciously provide for their manifold needs of spirit, mind and body and circumstance; and to all your servants in every land grant a fresh vision of Christ, a new willingness to lay down their lives and a never ending discovery of your almighty love, through Jesus Christ our Lord.   Amen.

At a Missionary Meeting

355 Sanctify our gathering together with your presence, O Lord. May your word quicken the words to be spoken, your Spirit quicken the hearts that shall receive them and your love unite

us in a community of loving concern: that the place which this work has in your holy will and mighty purposes may be faithfully mirrored in the life of your church; through Jesus Christ, our Lord.   Amen.

356 We thank you, Lord, for your special call to overseas service and for those who have answered it. We pray that their work may receive much blessing from you, that they may serve you faithfully and also see fruit from their labours: that many may be won from ignorance, superstition and bondage and brought into the light and freedom of the good news of Jesus Christ, for his sake.   Amen.

357 We thank you, Father, for Jesus Christ our Lord and for giving his church the work of spreading the gospel and proclaiming his death and resurrection. Be with all who are his witnesses: missionaries in other countries, ministers and other workers in this land; youth leaders and teachers in day school and Sunday school and all Christians everywhere. Make and keep them faithful to you, true to their message and full of love for the world and its people, for Jesus Christ's sake.   Amen.

358 O God, your gospel has the strength to set free those who are entangled and imprisoned by their own sins. Grant power to every member of your church that being ambassadors for Christ, they may so speak of him, crucified, risen and alive today, that many may come to share in the glorious freedom of your children; through the power of his name and for the sake of his name.   Amen.

Missionary Families

359 O God our Father, you have told us of our great responsibilities towards our children and you have also told us that if we love our children more than you, we are not worthy of you. Guide missionary parents as they seek to bring up their families and surround the children with your love,

especially when they are at school far away from their parents: for Jesus's sake.   Amen.

360   Heavenly Father, you call men and women to preach the unsearchable riches of Christ: be at this time with all those known to us who are sharing with others the good news. Be their companion in loneliness, their strength in weakness, their inspiration when the work is hard or dull; and grant them the joy of seeing the fruit of eternal life, both in themselves and in others: for Jesus Christ's sake.   Amen.

Ministry to the Jews

361   God of Abraham, God of Isaac, God of Jacob, may your ancient people the Jews also see in you the God and Father of our Lord Jesus Christ and find in him their great Messiah and their own true fulfilment; for truth and mercy's sake.   Amen.

362   We thank you, Lord, for the mystery of your covenant with the Children of Israel: for the commandments of your law and the sure word of prophecy proclaimed among them for their good and ours; and for the fullness of grace whereby the Word, both of law and prophecy, was made flesh and dwelt among them, in Jesus Christ our Lord.

We pray that all men everywhere may look unto him and be saved and particularly at this time we pray for all Jews who do not yet see in him the crowning glory and fulfilment of their faith.

Grant that the incarnate, crucified, risen and ascended Lord may be so presented to them in the power of the Holy Spirit that they may find eternal life in him and tell it out among the nations that this Lord is God.

Remove from the hearts of all Christians the ignorance, apathy or prejudice which negates their gospel and may the whole church be informed with a glad and lively understanding of your will.

Bestow your special blessing upon all engaged in the specialist ministry of Christ among the Jews and crown their

labours with abundant fruit; through Jesus Christ our
Lord.   Amen.

363   Forgive us, Lord, because Christian people have so often
persecuted the Jews and driven them away from Christ. Bless
all those who today, by word and deed, are trying to tell them
of his love, and help us each one to play our part, through
Jesus Christ our Lord.   Amen.

364   O God our Father, we thank you for inspiring Hebrew
writers to give us the Bible and Hebrew prophets to prepare
the way of Christ. We thank you for the Jewish disciples who
were the first Christian missionaries and preachers of the
Good News. We thank you, above all, for Jesus, your Son,
who was born to a Jewish mother. Help us to repay so great a
debt by doing all we can to send the message of Jesus back to
the Jewish people who first gave it to us and yet today know
so little of Jesus and his love: for his name's sake.   Amen.

The Church in Closed Lands

365   O Lord Jesus Christ, you open so that none shall shut and
shut so that none shall open: we cry to you for your own
people in those countries which men have tried to close to
your voice. We thank you that they are open to your Spirit
and your love; to the message of the Bible, which cannot be
bound, and to the church which cannot die. We pray that you
will strengthen this part of your church. Grant to its leaders
and all its members a new reliance on you to whom all power
is given, and a new commitment of themselves to share the
gospel with others before it is too late: for the sake of your
kingdom and your glory.   Amen.

366   Heavenly Father, we thank you that through the faithful
witness of Christians from other lands the gospel was brought
to this country and that through the faithfulness of others it
has been handed on to each successive generation and so to us.
Bless those who do not have this heritage or who lack the
freedom to enjoy it and make your presence and our prayers

very real to those who live in countries where the faith is suppressed, that seeing him who is invisible they may endure. Amen.

See also prayer 15.

Other Religions

367 Heavenly Father, help us to be willing to learn more about the world's religions, so that we may understand our differences, share our common convictions and go forward in faith to learn more of the truth as it is revealed in Jesus Christ our Lord. Amen.

368 Lord of all truth, make us sensitive and humble in our approach to all men. As we learn of their search for truth within the terms of other religions, help us also to see your search for them. Grant that by your Spirit and through the obedience of your disciples, what they have learned of you and your love may find its fulfilment in Christ, through whom alone we come to the full knowledge of yourself: God blessed forever. Amen.

369 Lord of all truth, make us sensitive and humble in our approach to modern secular man. Help us to understand his confusion, and appreciate his quest. Help us to respond to his cry and serve him with care and understanding. May your Holy Spirit so guide us to interpret your truth that many come to find in you their purpose, their meaning and their life: through Jesus Christ our Lord. Amen.

Missionary Societies in a New Age

370 We thank you, Lord, that the dream of missionaries of old has in part been realized and that your church has been planted in every land. Help the missionary societies of our church to understand your will for the whole church in this new age and direct them into the work which shall express it. And as we thank you for the dedication of the pioneers of missionary endeavour, we pray that your church, under the guidance of

the Holy Spirit, may face the challenges of a different world order while still looking for the day when your kingdom shall be acknowledged in the lives of all men: through Jesus Christ our Lord.   Amen.

Parish Missions

371 Risen Lord Jesus, we remember the way in which you called the disciples to be with you and how you sent them out, two by two, with your authority to speak about God and your power to cast out of men's hearts all that makes for death and destruction. Bless our desire to bring your message to this parish. Help us first to dwell with you and may it be your voice in our hearts which shall bid us go forth. And just as you rejoiced in the simplicity of your first disciples and through this saw the power of darkness fall, so give to us that uncomplicated response of children which you have taught us is the supreme achievement of the adult soul; for your dear name's sake.   Amen.

372 Eternal God, you have formed the universe and breathed life into mankind: call out from your church men and women to serve you in the world. Equip them with the gifts of your Holy Spirit and entrust to them the great task of bringing new life to the deadness which surrounds us; that there may be a new creation in the hearts of all who turn to your Son in repentance and faith, in whose name we pray.   Amen.

Camps, Holidays, Christian Holidays

373 We commend to you, Lord, all the members of this and other churches who are spending time this month in Christian camps and houseparties: give to those who lead them wisdom, patience, efficiency and love; to all the young people give health, safety and enjoyment; that everyone of them may be getting to know you better and that the eyes of some may be opened for the first time to your gift of eternal life in Jesus your Son: for his name's sake.   Amen.

Evangelistic Meetings

374 God of grace and mercy, open the eyes of the blind today;
breathe life where there is death; release those who are bound
by sin; and may the Holy Spirit take the truths of Christ and
impress them upon our hearts, our minds, our wills, that
hearts may be moved, minds convinced and wills challenged,
in his name.   Amen.

Missionary Power

375 O risen Christ: your wounds declare the suffering and victory
of God; we thank you for bursting the bonds of death.
    Look at us now.
    Look at our bonds.
    Look at the things which tie us down,
    which fasten our hands and hobble our feet,
    which stop us from walking in your ways,
    which stop us from doing your works,
    which tether us so tightly to the dead weight of past
failures.
    And as you have burst the bonds of death so burst these
bonds and set us free.
    Set us free from our pride; set us free from our sin;
    set us free from our fear; set us free from ourselves.
    Stand in our midst and in our hearts let us behold you.
    Lay on us your hands.
    Breathe into us your breath.
    Speak to us and may your speech be written into the
beating of our hearts.
    Speak to us and may your speech be carried in the motions
of our mind.
    So may the fire of your life fall upon us, that we may move
the mountains of irrelevance in our churches, and may have
that love without which faith is vain.
    So give us speech that each man may hear us speak in his
own tongue.
    So give us life that we may fashion anew in this generation
that army of disciples which can win the world for you.
    Look at us, Lord,

and may this body which you have bought by your death now be occupied by your resurrection and filled with your spirit: for your glory, for our peace, for the world, and for yourself.   Amen.

Before a Sunday School Teachers' Meeting

376 Lord of life, we thank you for coming into our lives and opening our eyes to the limitless love of our Father. We thank you for giving us a new quality of living which can never dwindle nor die because it is a part of your kingdom. We thank you for the children whom we teach and for whom we pray. Help us to make our worship with them worthy of your name, and be with us as we think about them now, for truth and mercy's sake.   Amen.

377 Dear Father, we thank you for our Sunday School and for the children trusted to our care. Make us sensitive to their needs, ready to listen as well as to talk. As we study and prepare lessons and as we teach, may our knowledge grow and our faith be deepened, through Jesus Christ our Lord.   Amen.

378 Lord, we thank you for our Sunday School where we can share with girls and boys our knowledge of your love and can worship together. Bless teachers with your wisdom and understanding. Bless children with a healthy appetite for your word. And grant that we may all grow in strength as active members of your family, to your honour and glory.   Amen.

379 Lord, may our knowledge of you grow daily so that we may be able to share with our children the reality of your love, through Jesus Christ our Lord.   Amen.

380 We thank you, Lord, for entrusting these children to our care. May we never blur their image of you by laziness or lack of love. Help us to teach them with care and imagination and according to their capacity to learn. Help us to feed them consistently with your word. And grant that they may know

Christ in spirit and in truth and in all things grow up into him, for his name's sake.   Amen.

381   Father, we pray for the children of our Sunday School. Help them to know you as their heavenly Father. Make them aware of the reality of your love in the person of Jesus. Help them by your Holy Spirit to learn to love you and to work for you. Give them courage to be true to you and to themselves with other people and at school. Be with each one and bless all, that they may be joyful members of your family, through Jesus Christ our Lord.   Amen.

For Confirmation Candidates

382   Father, we thank you for all the young people of our church who are to be confirmed. We thank you that they want to renew for themselves the promises made in their name when they were baptized as babies. Help them to keep these promises and to be lively members of your family through the power of your Holy Spirit.   Amen.

383   Father, we thank you for all the young people of our church who are to be confirmed. We thank you that in front of the whole congregation they want to declare their allegiance to you. Through the power of your Holy Spirit give them courage and love to show that they belong to you on every day and in all they do, through Jesus Christ our Lord.   Amen.

384   We thank you, Lord, for the growing purpose of our hearts and the growing resolution of our minds: grant us we pray the inner knowledge of Christ which will fulfil our being and glorify your name, through the power of the eternal Spirit, now and for ever.   Amen.

385   Risen Lord, help us to follow in the footsteps of your first disciples: like them, may we share in the physical hardships of your work; like them, may we share your concern for the needy; like them, may we share in your prayers; like them, may we learn the truth. Then, like them, may we become

willing workers in your kingdom, filled with the power of
your Holy Spirit, now and ever.   Amen.

For Godparents

386 Bless all who are called to be godparents, O Lord. Grant that
their love for you may provide the spiritual climate in which
young children may grow up and come to faith. Bless and
guide them in their own pilgrimage and may their lives
create in those for whom they pray a desire to be with Jesus
and to follow him; for his name's sake.   Amen.

THE SICK AND SUFFERING

A Nurse's Verse

387 Lord of all our aches and pain,
Help us so to use the brain
Thou gavest us, that we may share
The pain which others have to bear,
Thus linking them to us and thee.
Thyself the watch,
Help us to be minutes of thy time.

Grant, Lord, that we may bless
The hours when we receive
Rest from thy hands
And peaceful sleep.
We thank thee, Lord,
And vigil keep.

388 Merciful Father, help all who suffer pain of body or grief of
heart to find in you their help; and as Jesus suffered pain in his
body and healed it in others, help them to find their peace in
him and by your mercy be renewed in strength of body and
mind, through Jesus Christ our Lord.   Amen.

389 O God, the source of life and health, we pray for all who are ill. Give doctors and nurses skill to make them well again and grant that during their illness they may learn more of your love and care; through Jesus Christ our Lord.   Amen.

390 O Lord, we beseech you to strengthen those in pain and comfort those in sorrow and may the Spirit of Jesus, the great physician both of body and soul, be present in our parish, in our hospitals, and in the world.   Amen.

391 We thank you, Father, that out of suffering can spring compassion and caring, faith and endurance, joy from getting to know you, humility in knowing that you suffered, too. We bring before you now all those known to us who are in any kind of need. Give them courage and let your peace be in them; through Jesus Christ our Lord.   Amen.

392 One day, Lord, we shall understand why some people are physically handicapped while others walk and run and why life should be this way. But on the path to truth, dear God, teach us to help the afflicted and let their patience, hope and love spread over our embittered world; through Jesus Christ our Lord.   Amen.

393 Comfort and sustain all those in dire distress, O Lord, and give us all strength in our weakness, courage in defeat, wisdom in perplexity, and patience under provocation. Make us true where we are false and fill our hearts with your unconquerable love; through Jesus Christ our Lord.   Amen.

For the Aged

394 We pray, Lord, for those who have outlived the resources of their mind or body and for whom life is a burden and sorrow. Help them to know your presence in their need. Assure them afresh that in Christ their spirits may live more ardently than ever. And enable them, through loving you, to be a blessing to others and particularly to those who have the care of them. Grant them to know that while you call them to remain on

earth there is a purpose in their life and a grace for their living; through Jesus Christ our Lord.   Amen.

395 Eternal God, your Son Jesus Christ is the same yesterday, today and forever: we pray in his name for all who can now look back over many years of change, times of sadness and times of joy:

to those with a true sense of achievement in their lives grant the willingness to give you the glory;

to those with a sense of disappointment give the faith that your mercies are new every morning;

to those who have lost their faith and are lonely, grant the strengthening of their friendship with Christ;

to those who are losing their health or their faculties, grant the knowledge that their prayers are precious to you, and the grace to accept what seems too hard;

to those who can still influence others, grant youthfulness of mind and spirit, that their experience may be welcomed and valued;

and to those who are near to death grant the confidence to place their hands in the hands once pierced with nails, the hands of the risen Lord, stretched out now to meet them, the hands of him who is alive for evermore, even Jesus Christ your Son, our Lord.   Amen.

396 Lord Jesus, help of the helpless and companion of the lonely, we ask you to bless all those who are unable to leave their homes or to join in public worship. Grant that they may always be conscious of your presence with them, and of their oneness with the whole family of your church; and grant that with one mind and one voice we may all worship you, O Christ, reigning with the Father and the Spirit, one God for ever.   Amen.

The Mentally Ill

397 O God, the Maker of men's minds and Healer of their ills: bless all your children who suffer from mental illness; help them to trust you even on the darkest days; help them to

know you in their deepest need, and in your mercy release them from the causes of their sickness, that they may love and serve you with all their strength, with all their heart, and with all their mind: through Jesus Christ our Lord.   Amen.

398 O Lord, you shouldered the strain and stress of life and so we ask you to be with those who because of their burdens go down into the pit of disturbance and depression. When things seem black and hopeless stretch out your hand to hold them firm. Give them courage to climb upwards to the light of this world's day and of your love: through Jesus Christ our Lord.   Amen.

Thanksgiving for Our Bodies

399 O God our heavenly Father, we thank you for the wonderful way our bodies are made. We praise you for each breath we take, each step we take; for the gift of sight and the power to read; for minds that can observe and store up what they see. We thank you for hands that are skilful in doing work and for all the creative arts within us. And above all we praise you that our bodies are the temples of your own Spirit and that we are made in your image. Father, we give you praise: through Jesus Christ our Lord.   Amen.

For One in Pain

400 Lord, we pray for . . . in his pain. Help him to bear it patiently, to face it courageously, to accept it hopefully. Grant him your spirit of healing, your spirit of peace and endurance. May he place his whole trust and confidence in you, that in your light he may see light.   Amen.

Before an Operation

401 Lord, comfort and strengthen . . . as he prepares for his operation, and deliver him from all fear of the unknown. Bless the surgeons and all members of the theatre team. Help them to restore him to health again so that he may be better fitted to serve you and praise your name.   Amen.

402 Lord Jesus, grant . . . courage as he prepares for his operation.
Although he will be unaware of earthly things, may he feel
your presence with him, upholding and protecting him. May
he fear no evil, for you are with him.   Amen.

For Sick Children

403 Lord Jesus, God sent you into the world in the form of a little
child and you loved all children, taking them into your arms
and blessing them. Take these sick children into your care;
bless them and their anxious parents. Strengthen, too, the
hearts and hands of all who tend and nurse them.   Amen.

For the Elderly and Despondent

404 Lord Jesus, abide with those who are in the eveningtide of
their lives and make yourself known to them as you did to the
two disciples on the way to Emmaus, when it was toward
evening and the day was far spent. Be to them a companion
and a friend and bring them safe to their eternal
home.   Amen.

405 Lord we pray for those who are confined to bed in home or
hospital, particularly those who are lonely and friendless.
Give them a full and consoling sense of your presence and a
new vision of your fellowship and love for them.   Amen.

For the Dying

406 Have mercy, Lord Jesus, on all those who are dying. Bless
and support their families and all who care for them. May
they be enabled to see death as the gate of everlasting life and
be assured that, whether they wake or sleep, they are still
with you.   Amen.

For the Disabled

407 Lord, we are all disabled. We are disabled in spirit when we
do not love our neighbour as ourselves; we are disabled in

mind when our thoughts are purely selfish; we are disabled in
our bodies when our actions are inspired by pride.

In this awareness we pray for those who lack the powers of
mind or body we take for granted. We thank you for the grace
by which they adapt to their limitations and transcend them;
we pray that we may help them and that they may enrich us.

And we remember that for the sake of all mankind Jesus
our Saviour was disabled, too. He bore our sufferings and
carried our sorrows; was pierced for our faults and crushed for
our sins.

Grant that his pain may bring us peace, that by his wounds
we all may be healed: through the steadfast purpose of your
saving grace, and in the name of your Son Jesus Christ our
Lord.   Amen.

At a Service for Mentally Handicapped Children

408 Lord, you have created all the world of nature: flowers and
trees, brooks and streams, all the animals and people. Your
spirit is alive in the beauty of all creation.

We thank you that these your injured children respond so
fully to all that is good and beautiful in that created world of
nature.

Our lives are enriched by the purity, openness and warmth
of the love these children give us. When they love us we are
given a brief, fleeting glimpse into the very depths of your
divine love. For this we also thank you.

We learn so much from the truthfulness and humility of
these your special children. It shames us and we plead
forgiveness and ask for the power to be more like them.

Lord, we should not be surprised that the warmth,
response, purity, honesty and humility we receive from these
children is so awesome. After all, you did warn us that unless
we become as little children we could not enter your
kingdom.

So, Lord, keep these children under the protecting shadow
of your love and make us more truly child-like until we all
come into your eternal presence, through Jesus.   Amen.

FOR THOSE ENGAGED IN
HEALING MINISTRY

409 Help our parish, Lord, to become more aware of its mission of
healing and to see you as the source of all health and
wholeness. By its fellowship, prayer and sacrament may our
church bring comfort, strength and consolation to those
whom we visit and for whom we pray.   Amen.

410 Almighty Father, bless those who care for the sick when they
are themselves exhausted. Help them to be understanding
and gentle even when they are tired and help us to care for
them as they care for others; through Jesus Christ our
Lord.   Amen.

411 Lord God, we thank you for all those who stretch out their
hands to heal: for scientists who, by research and experiment,
stretch out their hands to heal; for all doctors and nurses,
physiotherapists and social workers, administrators and
clergy, who stretch out their hands to heal. And we pray
especially for those who stretch out their hands to heal where
hospitals are few and resources are scarce. We thank you that
through our gifts of prayer and money we too are able to
stretch out our hands; through Jesus Christ our
Lord.   Amen.

412 Lord Jesus, you have shown and taught us how to pray; you
have shown and taught us how to heal; you have promised
that we shall do great things in your name, through the
power of your Holy Spirit: break down all barriers between us
that hinder healing and release the power of your Holy Spirit
to flow through our hands, for your name's sake.   Amen.

413 Great God of love, we thank you for Jesus who gives us the
power to be pure. Open the eyes of all men everywhere that
they may let his healing power work in their lives and cure
the disease of sin, for his name's sake.   Amen.

414 We pray for all who are ill, O Lord; make them aware of your presence; begin in them your healing work and may nothing impede its course: no bitterness, resentment or fear, no unconfessed sin or unloving purposes. May your healing hand bring cleansing, courage, life and health, through Jesus Christ our Lord.   Amen.

415 O heavenly Father, who has bestowed upon us the comfort of earthly friends, we ask you to bless all who are visiting patients in hospital today. Grant that their time together may be hallowed by your presence, so that all earthly love may be gathered up into the love of God and your kingdom made manifest to men in the homes of your people.   Amen.

416 Lord Jesus Christ, our Good Shepherd, who laid down your life for the sheep, give to hospital chaplains the grace they need to fulfil their charge. Fill them with love for the souls committed to their care; guide them by your Holy Spirit in their undertakings, that all they do may be pleasing in your sight.   Amen.

For Lay Visitors

417 Almighty God, bless the work of lay visitors who are serving the church in their visiting of the sick in homes and hospitals. With the help of your grace may they so minister that by the dedication of their lives and the power of their prayers many of those whom they visit may be made whole.   Amen.

418 Lord Jesus, equip me for my work as a sick-visitor. In my weakness be my strength; in my fear be my guide; in my anxiety my comfort. Grant me the joy of knowing that, unworthy though I am, I am sharing in your task of making men whole.   Amen.

419 Lord Jesus, help me to realize that it is what I am at the bedside that matters most, no matter how helpless I feel inside. I remember how your mother and the disciple whom you loved stood in silence at the foot of the cross and how

their very presence meant so much to you in your pain and suffering.   Amen.

420 Lord, help me to bring some meaning to those in pain. There are lots of questions for which I have no answers, but let me in some way be able to comfort them by pointing them to you, who on your cross made pain more bearable and its mystery more understandable.   Amen.

Thanksgiving for Those Made Well

421 We join today in thanking you, Lord, with all those who have been restored again to better health; for faith and patience granted to us; for healing, in body, mind and spirit; for the skill and friendship and generosity of others; for the possibility of prayer and the comfort of the Bible; for sins forgiven and pardon assured; and through it all, for your unfailing presence: we give you thanks and praise, through Jesus Christ our Lord.   Amen.

Medical and Surgical Research

422 O God our heavenly Father, Creator of our bodies and of all that exists; we thank you for the knowledge and skill of surgeons and doctors, and for the advances that have been made in combating disease. We pray that all those in the forefront of medical and surgical research may be guided both in the practical and ethical aspects of their work. May the good of the patients never be sacrificed for the sake of prestige or any other unworthy cause. May the side-effects and complications induced by some new treatments be seen and overcome. May all be done in the Spirit of him who went about healing all manner of sickness and disease among the people, your Son, Jesus Christ our Lord.   Amen.

For Psychiatrists

423 Lord of all power and might, bless those who try to heal the disordered minds of men. Teach them first to study the mind

of Christ and inspire them to love this study best of all. In their exploration of the minds of men help them to be so secure in their own grasp upon reality that their strength of will, soundness of purpose and wholeness of spirit, may sustain them in their toil and give them good success; through Jesus Christ our Lord.   Amen.

For the Bereaved

424 We remember, Lord, the slenderness of the thread which separates life from death and the suddenness with which it can be broken. Help us also to remember that on both sides of that division we are surrounded by your love. Persuade our hearts that when our dear ones die neither we nor they are parted from you. In you may we find our peace and in you be united with them in the glorious body of Christ, who has burst the bonds of death and is alive for evermore, our Saviour and theirs for ever and ever.   Amen.

425 Father, we thank you that your love can turn to good the accidents and disasters of life and that through your Son Jesus, you have taught us that death is not an end but a beginning of a new life.

We give thanks for the life of... who has been taken from us. Comfort (his) family and friends; draw them closer to you; teach them and us in our sorrows and difficulties to lift our hearts to you and bring us all to meet again in your heavenly kingdom, for the sake of him who lived and died and rose again, that he might prepare a place for us, your Son, Jesus Christ our Lord.   Amen.

426 Father in heaven, you have called to (his) everlasting home (Name).

This mortal man you have clothed in immortality; to a body born to perish you have given an imperishable glory. We thank you, Father, that we have seen your goodness in this your servant; we thank you, Father, that now he sees you face to face.   Amen.

427 O God our Father, we pray for those whose life is saddened by
the death of a relative or friend. Be with them in their
loneliness and give them faith to look beyond their present
trouble to Jesus, the One who died and rose again and who
lives for evermore. Amen.

428 We pray, Lord, for those whose life has been shattered by
bereavement. Grant them the strength to meet the days
ahead with courage and patience, without resentment or
self-pity. May they be assured of a joyful reunion with those
they love and be confident of your continual presence and
fatherly care. Amen.

429 Lord Jesus, please be very near those who have been bereaved
of a loved member of their family. When we visit them, act
through us, so that we may have the courage to speak words
of comfort and truth to them. May they find the hope and
peace they need in you, the Resurrection and the
Life. Amen.

For Broken Homes and Broken Hearts

430 'The Lord is close to the broken-hearted and saves those who
are crushed in spirit' (Psalm 34:18).
   We pray for broken homes; for teenagers torn by doubts
and disillusionment; for old people bewildered by infirmities
and lack of human contact; for sick people fearful of the
future; for those who mourn.
   Lord, we claim your promise to be near the broken-hearted
and to save the crushed in spirit. Use us as channels of your
healing power. We thank you, Lord. Amen.

After a Disaster

431 Lord of compassion and power, be with those who have
survived this disaster: minister to their needs of mind and
spirit, body and circumstance; heal those who are hurt; give
peace to the dying; comfort and support the bereaved; and to
all who are working to bring relief and restore order, give

strength and resilience to do their work well; for the sake of
Jesus Christ our Lord.   Amen.

THE UNDERPRIVILEGED

432 Dear Lord, look down upon the starving world, your world:
upon the homeless men, the widowed women, the children
desperate for bread. Lord Jesus, take and save and feed us all.
Pour down your manna, your love, your life, yourself. Have
pity upon those who fast: have pity on us who feast. Pity
them, the pitiful, and us the pitiless. Have mercy on their
starving bodies and our starving souls.   Amen.

433 Have mercy, O Lord our God, on those whom war,
oppression or famine has robbed of homes and friends. Guide
us and all men as we seek to show them the love of Christ by
our prayerful concern and practical action; for his
sake.   Amen.

434 Forgive us, Father, that we are so eager to make our own lives
comfortable whilst others must suffer hunger and want. Bless
the little we have done and multiply it, in your mercy, to
serve the needs of many unknown to us, but known and loved
by you. May some give thanks to you, as we do now, for all
your love and care: through Jesus Christ our Lord.   Amen.

435 Grant to your afflicted children, O Lord, patience under their
sufferings, discipline in their affairs, hope in their hearts,
peace in their minds; and grant to us who have enough of this
world's goods, so to share our substance and our skills, that in
our day and age we may see all men enter fully into the
inheritance which is their birthright; through Jesus Christ
our Lord.   Amen.

The Starving

436 For all who are starving, O God, we ask your saving grace.
Move us to answer our own prayer at least in part by giving

money to those now trying to bring them practical help. Move the governments of the world to plan wisely and generously for the long term relief of all such chronic injustice and strengthen and inspire all whose lives are spent in bringing first-aid and food to mankind maimed by hunger: through Jesus Christ our Lord.   Amen.

437   Almighty Father, Giver of life and health, we beseech you for the millions of people who suffer from hunger. We acknowledge the richness of your bounty towards us and we pray for grace to show our thankfulness by seeking to relieve the needs of those who are in want. We ask this in the name of him who is the bread of life, your Son, Jesus Christ our Lord.   Amen.

438   We cry to you, O Saviour, for the homeless and the hopeless; for those who have no work, no clothes, no food. We cannot always hear their cries, but you can hear them, even when they do not know to whom they cry. We pray that you will be with them to rescue them and that you will be with us to drive us to their aid; for your own name's sake.   Amen.

439   O God, it is your nature to be generous: we confess to you our share of the guilt for a world of hungry families and homeless peoples. Forgive us for our lack of concern for them; forgive us for our self-centred living and spending; forgive those who blame you for their failures. Grant that this week those who have given nothing will start to give; those who have given something may give more; that both our church and our nation may give due place to the cries of those who have nothing to eat and nowhere to live; for the sake of Jesus Christ our Lord.   Amen.

Refugees

440   O Lord, have pity on those who today live in stables as you did and those who because of persecution take refuge in another land. We know you care for them, because you

yourself were once one of them. Help us to care too and so fulfil your law.   Amen.

441 Lord, make us more thankful for what we have received; make us more content with what we have; and make us more mindful of other people in need. We ask it in the name of him who lived in poverty, our Saviour, Jesus Christ our Lord.   Amen.

442 Lord Jesus Christ, you have taught us that we cannot love God and money and that all our possessions are a trust from you. Teach us to be faithful stewards of our time, our talents and our money, that we may help others and extend your kingdom, for your name's sake.   Amen.

443 O God, rich in mercy, your Son showed how hard it is for rich men to enter your kingdom; guard us from the temptation to use money wrongly; save us from selfishness, carelessness, and waste; deliver us from the love of money which is the root of all evil; help us to use properly what has been entrusted to us, to spend wisely and to save wisely, that neither poverty nor riches may hinder our Christian discipleship. And for those who have large sums to handle and great policies to decide, we ask that you will make them efficient, fair and strong to resist temptation; through Jesus Christ our Lord.   Amen.

The Victims of Vandalism and Crime

444 In this world, O Lord, the violence of a few strikes random victims among the many. We pray to you for these victims: all those who have been physically hurt; all those who have been robbed of personal treasures; all those who suffer reactions of bitterness and fear. O Lord Jesus Christ, your perfect life met death by violence and was not extinguished: so enter the hearts and minds of all victims that frailty may give way to your strength, loss to your gain, bitterness to your total and victorious love; for your name's sake.   Amen.

Immigrants

445 O God of all the nations, show us how to use our country for the benefit of mankind. Make our hearts to be sound in love and truth. Guide those who frame our laws. Teach us how to integrate into our society people from other lands. And may no difficulty blind us to the value of every human being, declared by Christ and written into history by his blood, for whose sake we pray. Amen.

446 Your Son, O God, was an immigrant into this world and so we ask you to bless all who move from the land of their birth to live in another. Guard and guide those who go from this land to live overseas. Guard and guide those who come from distant countries to live in this. And may loved ones abroad and strangers at home all be enabled to form new friendships and build a new world; through him who makes all things new, even Jesus Christ our Saviour and our Lord. Amen.

SOCIETY

447 'Let justice roll on like a river, righteousness like a never failing stream' (Amos 5:24).

O God of love, you have always required that man should be just: forgive our complacency and lack of care; forgive us for burying our heads in the Welfare State and believing that all is well with the poor, the hungry and the handicapped. In a society where those who shout loudest are best rewarded, open our eyes to the injustice around us and help us to give up ourselves, our time, our comfort and our possessions, in the service of others and of yourself: through Jesus Christ our Lord. Amen.

Employers

448 Lord Jesus, we ask you to give to all employers the strength to cope with the problems and difficulties inherent in their job. Give them the grace to listen patiently, see things clearly,

and act with wisdom; and help them to show your understanding and justice to all men: for your name's sake. Amen.

Shop Stewards

449 Lord Jesus, you once worked with your hands at the carpenters' bench and know the difficulties of a working day: bless those who represent their fellow workers' needs and meet with their employers in their name. May they see the problems clearly and try to solve them in the spirit you have shown to man, for truth and mercy's sake. Amen.

Trades Unions

450 God our Father, we thank you for the trades unions and for all that they have achieved in the past to improve the wages and conditions of workers. We ask you to bless all union leaders that they may use the great powers they possess wisely and well and contribute to that justice in industrial relations which is essential to the wellbeing of all. And to all Christians with positions of responsibility in the unions give your guidance that they may bring glory to your name, through Jesus Christ our Lord. Amen.

Industrial Relations

451 Almighty and everlasting God, we pray for all who work in industry. Bless all meetings between employers and employees. Remove all bitterness, distrust and prejudice from their deliberations. Give to all a spirit of tolerance and an earnest desire to seek for justice and for truth; that all may work together for the common good, through Jesus Christ our Lord. Amen.

Work

452 Thank you, Lord, for the gift of work and for the strength in which to do it. Thank you for our brains and our senses and

the strength in our limbs and bodies. Help us to use them well for you; to work well with other people and to make the place where we work a happier place. Help us to make the work of others easier and more pleasant and be with all those who find work difficult or dull or full of arguments. Bless those for whom we work and those who work for us: in the name of Jesus the carpenter, who is our Saviour.   Amen.

Those Who Work at Holiday Times

453 O God our Father, at this holiday time we pray for those who must work in order to maintain the essential services of our country: for doctors and nurses; for the police; for those who maintain the supply of gas and electricity and water to our homes; for those who maintain public transport. Bless them and the families from whom they are separated and may they all know the nearness of Christ, for his name's sake.   Amen.

For the Unemployed

454 We commend to you, Father of mercies, all who suffer through unemployment; all who would work if they could, but whose labour seems not to be needed. Provide for them and their families, we pray. Grant that no bitterness of mind may blot out your love from their lives. And help those in authority to give them the means of earning their living again; for the sake of that workman who was your only Son, Jesus our living Saviour.   Amen.

For Those Who Live Alone

455 Father of all, whose will is that your children shall become one flock within one fold, bless all who are also called to live alone. Help them to grow in the knowledge of Christ's body, the church, drawing from it and giving to it the treasures of love and the fruits of the Spirit, to their own comfort, protection and good, and to the glory of your name.   Amen.

A Countryman's Prayer at a Time of Loss

456 Almighty God, across our homes, in these times, a cold wind has blown: colder than the fell in winter, cold circumstances that leave us numb. And now we come to you, great Shepherd. Be unto us a strong wall: shelter us, O Lord, in these days.

We reach out to you: protect and succour us, O Lord.

Stretch out your strong arm: lift it up and say, 'Enough'.

Open up the roads of blessing to this community; give us faith, and hope and love.

We wait for spring; we wait for you; through Jesus Christ our Lord. Amen.

Thanksgiving for Safety in Hard Weather

457 Almighty God, Father of all mercies, we praise and thank you that in the midst of this hard weather you have protected your children and brought them safely home. Grant courage to those who have lost much; grant thankfulness and humility to those who have been spared; let neighbour continue to help neighbour under your kindly eye; through Jesus Christ our Lord. Amen.

For Farmers Facing Retirement

458 Heavenly Father, we pray your blessing on those we know who are facing the crisis of retirement; moving home; selling long-used things; uprooting themselves, perhaps, from sights and sounds to which they have been married for so long.

Grant them that spirit which sees this world as a place in which we are but travellers. Comfort them as only you can: for your Son Jesus Christ left his home to stay with us; then left to prepare a place for us.

So grant us all in later years a faith that gives us sight to see our home waiting for us, suited and prepared for our everlasting use, through Jesus Christ our Lord. Amen.

Redundancy

459 Bless, O Lord, all those who at the height of their powers have been deprived of their jobs. Help them and their families to adjust to this demand and deprivation and enable them in their crisis to work together as a loving and courageous team. Grant that all who lose security of employment may find an inner security in Christ, and, always being active in his service, may be led to full employment once again. And to this end we pray that governments and industry may plan humanely and well, so that by serving God men may master their fate, through Jesus Christ our Lord.   Amen.

Starting a Job after Leaving School

460 O God, our Creator and Preserver, we thank you for the strength to start new things. Guide and encourage those who are leaving school to start work. Help them to get used to new ways, new ideas, new people; give them wisdom to know what is right and good and the courage to do it; and may they do their work knowing that it is for you and that you are with them; through Jesus Christ our Lord.   Amen.

Leaving School without a Job

461 We grieve, Lord, that we have so ordered society that so many young people can find no work when they leave school. Save them from despair; help them to take the opportunities which come their way; sustain in them the spirit of enterprise and adventure; and by the unfailing endeavours of many people may ways be found to harness their strength to the needs of mankind, through Jesus Christ our Lord.   Amen.

The Use and Understanding of Money

462 Help us and all people, dear Lord, to understand the purpose and place of money in our life. Keep before us the peril of loving it. Help us to make it our servant and never our

master. And let neither the lack of it, nor the possession of it, in any degree loosen our grasp upon reality, which is ours through love of Jesus Christ our Lord.   Amen.

A Litany for Our Work

463 Let us remember that the first recorded command given to man was to work. Let us ask God's forgiveness for the times when we have considered our work as drudgery rather than as a gift from God.
Lord in mercy: hear our prayer.
Let us pray for all employers that they may carry out their responsibilities with justice and integrity. Let us pray for the members of this congregation who are employers.
Lord in mercy: hear our prayer.
Let us pray for all who are employed by others; that they may give good and honest work. Let us pray that Christians at work may seek above all to please God by their work.
Lord in mercy: hear our prayer.
Let us pray for the Trades Union Movement, thanking God for all that has been achieved by it. Let us pray for its leaders that they may exercise their great powers wisely and responsibly.
Lord in mercy: hear our prayer.
Let us pray for all those with whom we are brought into relationship by our work. Let us pray for our colleagues. Let us pray for those who serve us week by week: the postman, milkman, refuse collectors, shop assistants and all like them, upon whom we depend so much.
Lord in mercy: hear our prayer.
Let us pray for those whose work is dull and monotonous; for those whose work is dangerous; for those whose work causes them to be separated from their families for long periods; and for those whose work brings them into situations where they are greatly tempted.
Lord in mercy: hear our prayer.
Let us pray for those who cannot work; for those who cannot find employment because they are coloured immigrants; for

those who are disabled; and for those who have retired.
Lord in mercy: hear our prayer.

Professional Sport

464 We pray, Lord, for all engaged in professional sport as
players, administrators and businessmen. Help them to see
their work as part of a wider life and help them to remember
that all life comes from you. May they set for themselves the
highest standards of personal and professional behaviour,
both on the field and off, and for all who follow their fortunes,
may they provide an example to help make the heart of this
great nation sound, through Jesus Christ our Lord.   Amen.

465 We pray, Father, for all who engage in sports and contests for
their own pleasure and the entertainment of others. We pray
that they may be kept from harm and injury. We ask that
through their knowledge of the laws of the game they may see
that there are greater laws; that through their experience of
training and discipline they may see that there is a nobler
discipline; that through their desire for victory they may be
directed to the greatest triumph of all and the goal which is
Christ, the Saviour of the world, for his name's
sake.   Amen.

Drug Addicts

466 Lord Jesus Christ, you did not come to condemn the world
but to save men: look in mercy upon all drug addicts. Forgive
the actions which have brought them into captivity. Release
them from their craving for the next dose. Give them the will
to accept a cure, where one is possible, and restore them to
the blessings of a healthy life; for your tender mercy's
sake.   Amen.

467 O God, you created the raw material of drugs not to cause
suffering but to relieve it: we give thanks for all medicines
and for the inspiration and skill of those who discover and
administer them. We thank you for the relief from pain

brought by powerful drugs and the psychiatric insights
secured by the proper use of others. In our concern about their
misuse may we never fail to thank you for the good which
drugs can do; through Christ, the Healer of
mankind.   Amen.

468   Be with all those, Lord, who are tempted to take drugs: help
them to realize that not all experience is good, that not all
examples are to be followed, that not all pleasures herald joy
and bring enrichment. Give them a true knowledge of what
addiction really means and above all give them such an
experience of yourself and your love that they will want no
artificial substitute; through Jesus Christ our Lord.   Amen.

469   Lord Jesus Christ, who promised perfect liberty to those who
trust you, we cry to you for those who are at this moment
enslaved by their own need of drugs. Raise up men and
women with the skills to assist them and the capacity to give
them the care they need. Turn back those young people who
have already begun the drift towards addiction. Help us to
see how we may bear one another's burdens; and for those for
whom treatment has come too late, grant your mercy, the
awareness of sin, the awareness of yourself and peace at the
last.   Amen.

470   Strong Son of God, who came to set men free, be with those
who falsely worship freedom; save them from the slavery of
self regard; conquer their hearts; make them your willing
slaves; and so grant them the great freedom for which they
were made; for your great name's sake.   Amen.

471   We pray, O Lord, for the destitute who lack the will to accept
official aid. Help us to find a place for them other than the
street. And where official help fails may the church of Christ
succeed, for Jesus's sake.   Amen.

Vandalism

472   O God, we thank you for the beauty and health which exists

in the middle of cities and we pray for those who cause senseless destruction; for vandals who destroy property and amenities and who, by creating anger, suffering and suspicion, attack the health of the community.

Forgive us, Lord, for our own disobedience, we whose instinct is to condemn when your command is to forgive.

Forgive all, Lord, whose lives have been bent by ugliness, lack of love and lack of purpose, until the urge to create has become the urge to destroy.

Forgive us, Lord, for our part in permitting the evils of the city and the evils of the big estate and help us to share with others that power which can alone transform the human spirit and make it gloriously yours; through Jesus Christ our Lord. Amen.

DEPRIVED YOUNG PEOPLE

(Over half the number of convicted criminals each year are under the age of 17. The average age is 14½. Many of them are brought up in areas where they are herded together with little else to do and crime is an accepted part of life.)

473 Father of purity and light, goodness and love; with you there are no shades of gray or passing shadows: we bring before you the many young people who by accident of birth live often in the shadows; some without a father, some with parents who are mentally ill; some bursting with stifled intelligence, some innocently caught up with a bad gang; those in detention; those who are slaves to drink or drugs from an early age.

Father of light, allow that great light to shine through us on the people who walk in darkness; through Jesus Christ the light of the world. Amen.

Unloved Children

474 Look in mercy, Lord, upon all children born and reared in families where they are not loved: upon all who for lack of human love grow up unable to believe that God is love, and

for all who are destructive in their deeds in order to exact their vengeance or to cry for help.

Grant that the Christ who won the hearts of children, the hearts of parents and the heart of a dying thief, may win his victory in the hearts of all men everywhere, for his great mercy's sake.   Amen.

475 Lord of glory, born in a backyard stable, laid gently in a feeding trough full of straw: for our sakes you became poor. We bring to the heart of your compassion those who today live in squalor which insults the dignity you gave to man: the old lady lying amongst the rain drops which pierce her roof; the family in the slum whose children sleep in the drawers of an old chest; and the millions throughout the world who live in shanty towns or worse, without water taps or sewers. Lord of glory, give us the spirit of your love, never to rest complacent in our luxury, but to care, and to care, and to care: for your glory.   Amen.

Boredom

476 O God, you have made our life a sphere of endless interest and set us in a universe of marvellous diversity: save us from the selfishness which limits our interests; save us from building boredom into our industrial work; save us from building towns which are tedious to live in. Renew in us a vision of your kingdom and give us the will to seek it in lives, in the planning of industry, in the design of our towns, in the development of our culture and in the ordering of our world: that being caught up in your great purposes our affections, our will and our imagination may spring to endless life in the service for which we were born, through Jesus Christ our Lord.   Amen.

For Those in Prison

477 We pray, O Lord, for all those who have been imprisoned for crimes against society. Care for them in their many different needs. To hardened criminals grant repentance; to the

penitent give peace; to the confused give light; to all who suffer through separation from their families, give comfort. Renew the hope and love of married people; turn the hearts of parents to their children and the hearts of children to their parents and reunite them in your healing peace. And be so present, O Lord, in the prisons of our land that many may call upon you and be made whole and free in Christ our Lord.   Amen.

A Litany for Those Who Are, or Have Been, in Prison

478 We pray first for those who are responsible for the maintenance of law and order in our community; for those who administer justice in the courts; and for those who are the victims of crime, violence, and deceit:
> *Lord in mercy: hear our prayer.*

We pray for all prisoners, especially for those who are facing long sentences and those who have lost faith in themselves and their fellow men and have little hope for the future:
> *Lord in mercy: hear our prayer.*

We pray for young people; for those who have already come up against the law in borstal institutions and approved schools; for those on probation and for those on the fringe of delinquency; and we pray for parents, teachers, youth leaders, clergy and all who try to help boys and girls to escape from the sordid and the second rate, and to find a true purpose in life:
> *Lord in mercy: hear our prayer.*

We pray for all those who have the custody and care of prisoners; for prison governors, chaplains, officers: we pray for the Home Secretary and for those who in the Prison Department direct the policy of the prison service:
> *Lord in mercy: hear our prayer.*

We pray for all those who have a special concern for the after-care of offenders: probation officers and those who share with them the work of after-care, the wardens of hostels and the employers of labour:
> *Lord in mercy: hear our prayer.*

We pray for those who have been released from prison; those

who have managed to make good and those who continue to find the going hard; and we ask that we may learn to be as forgiving of others as we trust God is forgiving of us:

Lord in mercy: hear our prayer.

We pray for ourselves as members of the community and we ask that right respect for law and order may not lessen our compassion and concern for those who have failed to live up to the accepted standards of our society:

Lord in mercy: hear our prayer.

Prison Officers

479 Bless all who work in the prison service, O Lord. Help them in their lives to express the strength of goodness. May they not reflect the cynicism and the sin to which they are exposed. And save them from meeting evil with evil. Give to them a balanced and happy outlook. Bless them in their homes and with their families and make them strong in faith and hope and love; through Jesus Christ our Lord.   Amen.

The Legal System

480 We thank you, Lord, for the law of the land: for its roots in your holy word; for its development over centuries of service to society; and for all who have sought to use it aright. Where it is faulty and weak, restore it in truth and usefulness; where it is badly administered, grant pardon and guidance. And renew in us, and in those who frame our laws, the knowledge of yourself, through which alone mankind may live in peace; through Jesus Christ our Lord.   Amen.

481 Bless all judges and magistrates, O Lord, and give to them the wisdom to see clearly and the strength to act rightly, through Jesus Christ our Lord.   Amen.

482 Bless all who are called to jury service, O Lord. Help them to do their work well, to have a quiet mind and to be at peace among themselves. Enable them to understand their own thoughts and to share them clearly; and lead them to that

common mind which will serve the cause of truth, through Jesus Christ our Lord. Amen.

Policemen

483 We pray, Lord, for our police forces. We thank you for their constant availability in routine care and emergency aid; for the protection they afford to people and property; for their work in the prevention and detection of crime; for their help with the dangerous flow of traffic on the roads; for the security they provide at public gatherings of every kind; for their care of the sick, the lonely and the lost. Strengthen them in that which is good; make them sensitive to the counsel which all men need; give them a happy relationship with the communities they serve; protect them in the dangers of their tasks; bless their families and their homes with love and peace; and give them a due reward for all their labours: through Jesus Christ our Lord. Amen.

484 We pray, Lord, for those communities where social deprivation breeds civil disorder and where policemen are resented and disliked. May the causes of discontent be rightly perceived; may the wider community play its part in removing injustice and redressing wrong; and while passions run high and people are hurt, grant courage and protection to the police and all men of good will, that violence may be contained and the innocent protected; through Jesus Christ our Lord. Amen.

For the Church in the Inner City

485 We thank you for the great cities of our land, O Lord; for their traditions of community life and social care; their industry and commerce; their culture, scholarship and faith; and for the ways in which they help to knit together the nation's knowledge of itself. We thank you for the ministry of your church in each of them, in good times and in bad, in peace time and in war. Bless that ministry now we pray, in times of redevelopment and change, that the light of life

might be a constant guide, through Jesus Christ our
Lord.   Amen.

TRAVEL AND TRAVELLERS

486 Lord Jesus Christ, you travelled once by hard and dangerous
roads; you drew near to your friends as they journeyed on the
way, both going along with them and sharing with them
your truth. Be present we pray with those who travel this
week; guard them in every danger; make them aware that you
are with them and bring them safe and well to where they
want to be: for your own name's sake.   Amen.

487 Lord God, you have taught us to love our neighbours as
ourselves: give to us and to all who use the roads—to drive, to
ride or to walk—consideration and care for others; that none
may suffer death or injury and that all who travel may go in
safety, peace and joy: through him who is the way, the truth
and the life, Jesus Christ our Lord.   Amen.

488 Lord, we pray for those who design cars and build them,
those who plan routes and build roads, those who direct
traffic and provide emergency services: grant to them vision
and wisdom and far-seeing care, through Jesus Christ our
Lord.   Amen.

Air Travel

489 We thank you, God, for giving men the spirit and the powers
which express themselves in flight: bless all who work with
aeroplanes that they may do their work well and for the good
of all. Bless those who design and build aircraft; bless those
who operate airlines; bless those who devise routes and
timetables; bless all aircrews and ground staff; and by your
blessing upon all these grant that all who travel by air may go
safely on their way; through Jesus Christ our Lord.   Amen.

SCIENTISTS AND SCIENTIFIC RESEARCH

A Researcher's Prayer

490 God, show me truth and beauty through this work. Give me
honesty and courage to retrace my steps from each blind
alley. Open my clouded understanding to the pattern behind
the tangled facts. Rescue me at the end from unwarranted
pride, and grant that the insight you will give may not be
misused by me or others; through Jesus Christ our
Lord. Amen.

For Fellow Members of a Research Team

491 Thank you, God, for this research team. We are so different
in our skills and in ourselves: the technician and the scholar,
the mathematician and the intuitive thinker, the washer-up
and the brewer of tea. We care about the truth and we are
grateful when it dawns upon us. Help us also to care about
one another; to the gift of truth add the gift of love; through
Jesus Christ our Lord. Amen.

For a Right Use of Knowledge

492 We thank you, Lord, for this wonderful world with all its
resources: so much recently discovered, so much yet to be
found. We thank you for the trained minds and patient
personalities which harness nature's powers to human need:
for swift travel and instant communication; for research into
the causes and cure of disease; for space research into
unknown worlds. Accept our thanks, O Lord, and accept too
our penitence for the many ways we use our knowledge for the
destruction, suffering and despair of mankind, rather than
for the building up of life on earth in happiness and hope.

May your Holy Spirit pervade the minds of scientists and
politicians in every land and shape the desires of men and
nations, that your gifts may be a blessing not a curse, through
Jesus Christ our Lord. Amen.

Space Travel and Research

493 O Lord our God, the heavens declare your glory, the moon
and the stars which you have ordained; yet you have given to
men dominion over the world of your hands. We pray for the
safety of those who travel far beyond the earth, and ask that
the skill and knowledge of scientists and explorers may be
used for the benefit of all men and the glory of your
name.   Amen.

494 O God, the Creator of all, we thank you for the wisdom
which has set this world in so vast a universe. Help us to care
properly for this planet and to respond intelligently to the
mystery and challenge of the wider creation. We thank you
for the spirit of enquiry and adventure which helps man to
master his environment and we pray for those now engaged in
the exploration of space. Grant to them a motive which is
right, a will that is pure and the blessings of safety and peace
of mind. And so govern the minds of men and nations, O
Lord, that the knowledge which is won may be used for the
good of all and the harm of none; through Jesus Christ our
Lord.   Amen.

495 We thank you, Lord, for revealing to the eyes of searching
men still more of the wonders of creation. Teach us also how
to use the knowledge being won. Give to all who risk their
lives and loved ones the blessings of your peace and care and
may all who direct and carry out journeys into space grow also
in the knowledge of God their Saviour. And so guide the
desire of men and nations, O Lord, that space research may
bear fruits of peace in the affairs of men, through Jesus Christ
our Lord.   Amen.

ART AND ARTISTS

496 We thank you, God of creation, for the faculties by which we
may perceive beauty and the heart with which to love it. Give
us eyes to see and ears to hear each sight and sound which tells
of your love for mankind. And since you are greater than your

creation let us not be content to love your world without
much more loving you, through Jesus Christ our
Lord.   Amen.

497 O heavenly Father, you have filled the world with beauty;
open our eyes to behold your gracious hand everywhere, that
rejoicing in your creation we may learn to serve you with
gladness; for the sake of him through whom all things were
made, your Son Jesus Christ our Lord.   Amen.

498 We thank you, O God, for all the wonders you have made and
for the creative gifts you have given to man. We offer our
thanks in humility and gladness for all who use these gifts to
increase the richness of life; for the consecration of art to your
service; and for all things that help us to see the true nature of
your creation, through Jesus Christ our Lord.   Amen.

499 Almighty God, author of all beauty and goodness, forgive us
and all men for the misuse of your many gifts, both now and
in the past, through selfishness and ignorance. Forgive our
failure to exercise a proper care for these gifts, forgive us for
offering you things that are unworthy. Pardon our sins and
let your forgiveness open our eyes to new opportunities of
service and a new awareness of your glory; for the sake of Jesus
Christ our Saviour.   Amen.

500 O God, your Spirit in our hearts teaches us to desire your
perfection, to seek for truth and to rejoice in beauty:
enlighten and inspire all artists and craftsmen in whatever is
true, pure and lovely; that your name may be honoured and
your will done on earth, for Jesus Christ's sake.   Amen.

501 Almighty Father, may the Holy Spirit guide all Christian
groups concerned with the improvement of art; that in closer
cooperation their aims may be more fully achieved, through
Jesus Christ our Lord.   Amen

502 Loving Father, source of order and form in life: inspire us in
our work that we may constantly seek your guidance,

acknowledge your presence, and daily strive to serve you faithfully; for Jesus' sake. Amen.

503 O God our Father, you clothe the world in beauty, look with mercy upon all artists. Open our eyes that we may see with true vision; quicken our minds; guide our hands to interpret the beauty of your creation; and inspire us to convey your message to the world, through Jesus Christ our Lord. Amen.

504 Dear Father God, your blessed Son Jesus Christ showed compassion to those deprived of your good gifts: help us to enrich the lives of those starved of the enjoyment of beauty; that through our efforts, the wonders of your creation may be known more and more by all your children: through the same Jesus Christ our Lord. Amen.

MUSIC AND MUSICIANS

Thanksgiving for Music

505 Father, we thank you for the many ways we can express ourselves and particularly we thank you for the gift of music. We thank you for the way it can express every emotion: joy and delight; melancholy and sadness; wonder and worship; love and devotion. We thank you that music can soothe the soul and bring solace to those who mourn. And we thank you, too, that like the Israelites of old, we can make merry before you and show our joy in music and song, singing and making melody in our heart, through Jesus Christ our Lord. Amen.

Composers

506 Bless all those, O Lord, who compose music: those who take the sounds of the earth, the passions of the heart and the motions of the mind and bind all together in the mystery of music. Grant that in their work our souls may be touched by

your glory, for our blessing, and your praise, through Jesus
Christ our Lord.   Amen.

Musicians

507   O Lord Jesus Christ, your birth was heralded by angels' song,
your death for sinners is extolled by the music of heaven:
grant that those who use voices and instruments to show your
glory may also find in their lives that harmony which echoes
your praise: for your own name's sake.   Amen.

508   God our Father, we thank you for all those who have enriched
the world with music: for composers and conductors; for
singers and instrumentalists; for all those who, by your gift,
produce or interpret music and bring joy and beauty into the
lives of men and women, boys and girls and into the worship
of the church: through Jesus Christ our Lord.   Amen.

509   Lord, we ask your blessing on all those whose responsibility it
is to beautify the worship and praise of the church with music
and singing.
   Grant skill and patience to choirmasters and organists;
give to choristers a sense of reverence and of the importance of
their task; and give to us all who sing your praise, willing
hearts and minds to serve and glorify you, not only in psalms
and hymns, but in all aspects of our daily lives: through Jesus
Christ our Lord.   Amen.

510   We give thanks, Lord God, for our sense of hearing and for
the many sounds which please our ears. We thank you for
music, for instruments, and for singing voices. We also
praise you for the ability of music to express joy, sorrow and
love, and to add to our worship of yourself.
   We pray that you will enable those who sing and make
music to do so to your great glory, that we may appreciate
some new truth or beauty, unrealized before. We ask these
things in the name of Jesus Christ our Lord and
Saviour.   Amen.

THINKERS AND WRITERS

511 O God, the inventor of thought, the creator of speech, bless all who work with thoughts and words and ideas; enter into their thinking as inspiration, redeemer and guide; grant that their minds may grow upward into light and enable them to share that light with all mankind, through Jesus Christ our Lord.   Amen.

For Novelists and Dramatists

512 For human hearts and minds we thank you, Lord, and pray for those who tell the stories of their interplay. We ask you to bless all novelists, dramatists, poets and journalists and pray that in you they may find new dimensions of their minds, new powers for their pens and new worlds for men's desires; through Jesus Christ, the Lord of man's story and the end to which it moves.   Amen.

Mass Media

513 O God, your blessed Son Jesus Christ is the eternal Word in whom may be read the good news of creation: grant to all who speak or write what many hear or read, that love of truth which leads to love of God and that love of God which makes communication of thought a good and holy thing, through Jesus Christ our Lord.   Amen.

Discrimination in Reading

514 O God, there is more to read than time in which to do so: guide us in our choice of books, magazines and papers; and may the thoughts which enter our mind through the printed page increase our maturity and help the advancement of your kingdom, through Jesus Christ our Lord.   Amen.

MARRIAGE AND FAMILY LIFE

Engaged Couples

515 Thank you, Lord Jesus Christ, for enriching the wedding at Cana in Galilee, both by your presence and by your generous gifts: please also enrich those who are engaged to be married. Grant that no couple may be joined together unequally or wrongly; and grant that those whom you are calling to be married may grow in honesty, maturity and love for each other, and that their married lives may draw their strength and unity from you and reflect your glory to others.   Amen.

Penitence and Thanks in Married Life

516 Lord, we are sorry and we ask your forgiveness that sometimes we show lack of respect and understanding and love; that we neglect each other by neglecting to pray for each other; that we have often spoiled the perfect relationship you planned for us; and yet we also want to thank you for the happiness we have known together, for the sadness we have faced together, for the problems we have overcome together, for the love which you give us which is completely unspoiled; in the name of Jesus Christ.   Amen.

Newlyweds

517 O God, in your word you have compared marriage to the perfect union between Jesus your Son and the church his bride; be present we pray with all those newly married as they set up a new home together. Grant them lasting faithfulness to you and to each other; true unity with you and with each other; increasing love for you and for each other: that they may know that unless the Lord builds the house the builder's work is all in vain; and that you will make their homes places where others may meet with you; through Jesus Christ our Lord.   Amen.

At the Time of an Engagement

518 Lord, we thank you for the gift of love: the love of God for
man and man for God. And we thank you for human love
between man and woman. We pray that during the months
of engagement you will guide us in all our ways, in our
relationship to each other and in our preparations for the
marriage, so that on our wedding day we may give our whole
minds to the joy of the service and the gathering together of
those we love, through Jesus Christ our Lord. Amen.

Wedding Day

519 We thank you, Lord, for the dawning of this day and for your
love which is new every morning. We pray for those who are
to be married today and ask that you will give them great joy
in the fulfilment of their love. And we ask you to bless their
parents with a sense of your nearness, and a great
consciousness of belonging to each other; and to all who are
called to share their lives in marriage grant faithfulness to
their promise, through Jesus Christ our Lord. Amen.

A Baby in the Family

520 O God our Father, we marvel that you created the world and
all that is in it. The news of our child fills us with wonder and
joy at our part in your purposes. Confirm our hopes, we pray,
and teach us how to pray for our child even now. Prepare our
lives and our home so that the child may know your love from
the beginning. We thank you, in Jesus' name. Amen.

521 Thank you, Lord, for the safe arrival of our child and for the
care of doctors and nurses. We thank you for the gift of life
and we pray that our child may grow in wisdom and stature,
and in favour with God and men, after the pattern of Christ
and by his grace. Amen.

A Child's First Day at School

522 Lord, we thank you for this home where we are safe and happy. In our first adventures alone make us brave and true. Help us in our learning and may we find good friends and enjoy our new adventures, through Jesus who goes with us.   Amen.

A Child's Prayer at Night

523 Lord Jesus Christ,
in your arms tonight
help us to sleep
with our eyes shut tight.
Help us this and every day
to be deaf to Satan
and to hear what you say.   Amen

A Child's Prayer in the Morning

524 Dear Lord, may the love that is hidden in us be shown to others: to people we dislike, to ones who are not as lucky as ourselves. May we not be deaf to your voice; help us to understand you; help us to do what you say.   Amen.

Thanksgiving for Children

525 Dear Father, we give you thanks for children and particularly for those who are committed to our care. We thank you for their innocence, their laughter, their loving, and their unquestioning trust in us. Help us, Lord, by word and deed to give them a simple and steadfast faith, a loving heart and a cheerful nature, that they may be equipped to be citizens of this world and the next, through Jesus Christ our Lord.   Amen.

Family Life and Fellowship

526 Father, we thank you that you have established us in families

so that we may live together, play together, work together, rejoice together and grieve together. But above all we thank you that we are able to be members of your family, the church, able through Jesus Christ to be your children, to share one another's burdens, rejoice in one another's blessings, and strengthen one another through the power of your Holy Spirit. Thank you for appointing a day each week when we can gather together for praise and worship and be renewed as a family by your Holy Spirit, through Jesus Christ our Lord. Amen.

Renewal of Vows

527 We thank you, Lord, that as we exchanged our promises you were listening. Grant us now your blessing: the blessing of the Father who cares for us and watches over us understandingly; the blessing of the Son, who taught us how to live faithfully and perseveringly; the blessing of your Holy Spirit who binds us together in heart and home. Amen.

A Housewife's Prayer for Contentment

528 Dear Lord, help us to be happy doing the work you give us to do, even if it is often monotonous. When the babies need to be fed, meals to be cooked and there is an everlasting war to be waged with the rising tide of toys and books and papers: give us the good sense to take time to stop and think of you and of your goodness, because this is the only way to peace and contentment; through Jesus Christ our Lord. Amen.

A Housewife's Thanksgiving

529 Thank you, Lord, for homes and families; thank you for our health and happiness; thank you for the good things and for helping us to cope with the times that are not so good. Thank you for your love and for life itself. Amen.

BROKEN HOMES AND FAMILIES

530 O Lord our heavenly Father, look mercifully upon those
whose lives have been shattered by the breaking up of their
homes. Grant to your children freedom from recrimination
and the strength to seek your will in every situation. Prosper,
we pray, all work of reconciliation that all may come to
acknowledge you, the only perfect Father, who with the Son
and Holy Spirit lives and reigns for ever and ever.   Amen.

531 O Lord God, we thank you for the gift of marriage; that gift
which leads to the height of shared joy or to the depths of
shared bitterness. We pray for those who have suffered hurt
in marriage; for those who have inflicted it and for those
whose greatest unhappiness stems from the closeness of their
partner. O Lord, it was in love that you created the
complexities of the human mind and it was with power that
you conquered the evil that invades it: bring wholeness to
those who are fragments and unity to those who long for it,
that we may all finally be united with yourself and with one
another.   Amen.

532 O Lord, we pray for all those who, full of confidence and love,
once chose a partner for life and are now alone after final
separation. May all receive the gift of time, so that hurt and
bitterness may be redeemed by healing and love, personal
weakness by your strength, inner despair by the joy of
knowing you and serving others, through Jesus Christ our
Lord.   Amen.

For Understanding Between Generations

533 Father of Jesus, give grace and understanding to all who live
in families. May the spirit of peace settle between parent and
child, brother and sister. May the young realize that the old
may be wiser than they. May the old see how many of the
young are trying to set up your kingdom on earth. And by
their harmony may they give glory to you, O Father, and to

the Son, through the one Spirit, O God, blest
forever. Amen.

534 O Father, and Maker of all things, we are the work of your
hands. Continue your work in us, that we may show forth
your righteousness to our children and our children's
children; for the love of your blessed Son, our Saviour Jesus
Christ. Amen.

For Children Who Lose Their Parents

535 Dear Lord and Father, we commend to your loving kindness
all children who have lost their parents. Give special
inspiration and grace to those who look after them in the early
moments of their loss. Give great love and joy to those who
care for them over the following years. And in and through
their bereavement help the children to trust you as their
heavenly Father, knowing that their earthly parents are in
your care and that those who care for them are sent by you to
take their place: so may they love and serve you all their days
and joyfully care for children in their turn, through Christ
our Lord. Amen.

For a Sick Child

536 Father of all, you know our grief and our anxiety. You know,
too, our love, our prayer, our hope. We pray for our child.
We thank you that he/she is your child too, and has a place in
your eternal and loving purposes. We pray for life, we pray
for health. And we pray that we may have wisdom to do the
right things during this time. We thank you that in your love
you allow only that which is good for your children. We
know, too, that you see beyond our own horizons in working
for the wholeness, healing and peace of us all. Help us to trust
you in all things, O Lord of life. Amen.

Before Bringing Children to Baptism

537 O God our Father, from whom every family on earth takes its

name; be present to bless the families of the children soon to be baptized as members of your church. Help the parents and the godparents to see the meaning of your saving gospel; to make the promises sincerely and heartily; to pray for their children; and to teach them of holy things; so that all may share in your gift of eternal life, through Jesus Christ our Lord.   Amen.

For Those Recently Baptized

538 Lord Jesus Christ, because you welcomed the little ones who were brought to you, we pray for those who were today added to the fellowship of your church. Guard them in health and strength as they grow up; help their parents to trust you and to make each home your dwelling; and use the children's work of this church to nourish their faith in you; for the glory of your saving name.   Amen.

Young People of the Church

539 O God our Father, bless we pray the young people of our church; keep them faithful to you when the world beckons in the opposite direction; guide them in the great decisions they have to take concerning a career and choice of marriage partner; and grant that in you they may find true peace, so that armed with your Spirit they may do great things for you, for the sake of Jesus Christ our Lord.   Amen.

Young Disciples

540 O God our Father, we praise you for those who in the past weeks have put their trust in Jesus Christ as their Lord and Saviour at camps, house-parties or missions, in this church or in their homes. May their faith grow, may their love increase and may they find encouragement and fellowship within the church. Help us we pray to give to all who have become your disciples the support of our friendship and our prayers, through Jesus Christ our Lord.   Amen.

SCHOOLS AND COLLEGES

541 Lord of all being, because our schools reflect the spirit of the age, imparting attitudes as well as knowledge, values as well as skills, we pray for the life of each school and its relationship to society. Grant that each community may turn to you for light upon its life and find in you the way which it should take and share the spirit of its quest with its children, those members of every society who are most impressionable and who have longest to live; we ask it through Jesus Christ our Lord. Amen.

542 Grant that our schools, Lord, may help the young to get knowledge, to keep it, to share it, to use it, in wisdom and in love, for the good of all and the praise of your name, through Jesus Christ our Lord. Amen.

Children Leaving Primary School

543 O Lord our heavenly Father, bless all who are leaving this school this term; watch over them, protect them, help them, encourage them. Keep them faithful in their prayers, loyal in their friendships, happy in their new schools. Help them to know that though they are leaving some of their friends they will be making new ones. Help them to remember that you are always near: through Jesus Christ our Lord. Amen.

For a School

544 Father, we hold before you in prayer our life together in this school. Help us to give to it of our best and to receive in turn the best it has to give. Teach us to know the joys of discovery, the warmth of friendship, the satisfaction of attempting and achieving and the demands of truth. Open for us week by week new windows on our world; increase our understanding of ourselves and others. May teachers and taught alike seek first your kingdom, to the good of this school and the glory of your name, through Jesus Christ our Lord. Amen.

A Teacher's Prayer

545 When the class is trying and the progress is slow; when our
duties are irksome and the time long; when our patience is
exhausted and we have no reserve: good Lord, help us.

From staff room gossip which profits nothing; from the
sarcastic word which is meant to sting; from lack of patience
and loss of temper: good Lord, save us.

A word of encouragement for the cheerful plodder; a word
of timely warning for the careless and idle; an even
disposition which refuses to be ruffled: good Lord, give to
us.   Amen.

A Pupil's Prayer

546 That which is worth knowing; that which is worth hearing;
that which is worth seeing; that which is worth believing:
give us grace to find. Give us this day our daily bread.

May I work hard as one who needs not be ashamed. Even
today may I learn something that interests and excites me.
Even today may I discipline myself to be careful and
thorough. Even today may I exert myself to the utmost of my
ability. Even today may I learn to seek after knowledge and
truth: today and every day.   Amen.

Teacher and Learner

547 May we explore together the territory of knowledge. May we
learn together the mysteries of truth. May we share together
the experience of beauty. May we join together in the joy of
physical activity. May we ever remember that you, the
Author of all knowledge, yourself Goodness, Truth and
Beauty, delight to share all experience with us: through Jesus
Christ our Lord.   Amen.

For Those with Exams Soon

548 We remember before you, O God of truth, all those students
and scholars facing examinations, especially those known to

us and those who know you. Grant that they may readily remember all that they have honestly learned and give a true account of their ability, so that whatever may depend upon the results they may willingly give their future to your disposing; through Jesus Christ our Lord.   Amen.

On Examination Day

549 Lord, we need your help. We need a calm mind: grant us your peace. We need a clear head: grant us your wisdom. We need to be careful: grant us your patience. We need to be inspired: grant us your enthusiasm. Keep us from all panic as we put our trust in your power to keep us this day.   Amen.

The Whole School Community

550 We thank you, Lord, for this school to which we belong: for its foundation and continuing life under your directing power; for all who work in it and for it. Thank you for the service given by teachers and pupils; by domestic and kitchen staff; by clerical staff and those who govern its business and by parents and friends: may all these work together for its common purpose.

We pray that individual gifts and talents may be discovered, developed and used for you and for the good of others: through him who as a man both learned with care and taught with power, Jesus Christ our Saviour.   Amen.

At the Beginning of Term

551 With grateful hearts we thank you, Lord, for the rest and enjoyment of our holiday; for the opportunity of being with family and friends; for time of recreation in mind and body.

May we start work again with cheerfulness and good will, resolved to use to the full our strength and ability. We ask this in the name of Jesus Christ our Lord.   Amen.

At the End of the School Year

552 Heavenly Father, we thank you for the term which is just finishing and we ask your blessing on the holidays about to begin. Help us to remember that their rest and refreshment are your gift. Help us not to spoil them by unworthy words or actions. May our holidays be happy and vigorous so that we come back renewed in body and mind; through Jesus Christ our Lord. Amen.

553 Lord, we commend to your care those who are leaving school this summer. Guide them in times of difficulty; preserve them in times of danger; help them in the work that they are to do; and keep them in health and happiness. May they freely share with others the gifts they have received here. We ask this through Jesus Christ our Lord. Amen.

For the School

554 Heavenly Father, we ask your blessing on this school. We are grateful for the lives and examples of all who have served here as teachers and learners and for the gifts of education and opportunity which are ours. Direct us in our work and play and grant that we may do things not just for our own advantage but for the common good; so that school and community may be the better for our lives; through Jesus Christ our Lord. Amen.

Before Lessons

555 Here we are, Lord: our school gathered together to worship you and to be glad together. We have enjoyed our holiday (or weekend) and learned lots more about your world and your people. Now help us to be ready to work at the things we do in school.

Be with all our teachers and helpers; be with our friends and with us, that this school may be a happy place.

If we have worries and troubles about our classes, our play times, our work, or unkind people, be very close to us and help us to cope.

Be with us now, Lord, as we go to our classes.   Amen.

556 Lord of heaven and earth, we call to you. We want to praise you but often we don't know how. We've enjoyed our breakfast. We've run along the road and shouted in the subway. We've played with our friends in the playground and talked to our teachers. But now we come here to be together, to be quiet, without any rush, to sing and pray: because you are in all the parts of our life, at home, at play and at school. We praise you, Lord of our lives.   Amen.

557 People, Lord, people everywhere. We hear trains rushing by, carrying commuters to their work. There is the roar of cars and lorries hurrying to the tunnel or the bridge to get their cargoes of people and goods to the city. The river is there, too, with people travelling up and down. So many people, milling about around us, Lord, in this big city. But we remember that this is your world, these are your people and we pray for them and with them—Lord, your people.   Amen.

The Work of Education

558 God, you are the goal of all knowledge, the source of all truth, our leader along the paths of discovery and learning. Direct with the spirit of wisdom the work of education in this and every land. Give to those responsible for its planning, organization and administration, insight and vision. May they have the humility to learn from experience and wisdom, to combine the old and the new; through Jesus Christ our Lord.   Amen.

At Examination Time

559 Heavenly Father, give your blessing to our work, that we may do it to your glory. May all our study be done honestly and faithfully. Give us strength, wisdom, and patience, and whether we succeed or fail, may our confidence in you and

your purposes remain; we ask this through Jesus Christ our
Lord.   Amen.

At a Staff Meeting

560 Father, we pray for harmony, as we seek to foster in this
school the natural spirit of good will. Help us to show our
pupils a true example; grant that the relations between all of
us here may be those of cooperation and affection; let personal
ambition be far from us and may we always regard it as our
chief privilege to serve you in this work: through Jesus Christ
our Lord.   Amen.

A Teachers' Service

561 Father, may your Holy Spirit guide and inspire us. Give us a
vision which will open to us clearer objectives; give us
courage to conquer our disappointments; give us love which
never fails.

Save us, in our work, from lack of discipline in mind or
body, from sloth and selfishness, annoyance and despair.
Show us how best we may carry out our task as teachers,
waiting always on your guidance; through Jesus Christ our
Lord.   Amen.

A Litany for the Young

562 Let us give thanks for Christ's revelation to us of God's love
for children and of their infinite value in his sight.
We thank you, O Lord.
For his tender compassion towards them; for his burning
indignation against those who do them wrong; for his deep
and overflowing love, drawing them with irresistible
attraction to himself; for his message of their nearness to the
Father of all.
We thank you, O Lord.
For the beauty of children and their joy in all beautiful
things, for their mirth and laughter and for the joy and light
they bring into the world.
We thank you, O Lord.

For their enthusiasm, their unbounding energy and their love of the heroic and adventurous; for their candid, generous trust in those around them and for their quick response to calls of love and service.

We thank you, O Lord.

O Lord forgive, because there are still children in need of care and love:

O Lord, forgive;

because homes are broken by selfishness, pride and greed:

O Lord, forgive;

because even in our affluence children remain in spiritual and moral danger:

O Lord, forgive;

because children continue to be exploited by the greedy and the lustful:

O Lord, forgive;

because children in many parts of the world suffer from disease and malnutrition:

O Lord, forgive;

because many children are homeless and many are not taught to read or write:

O Lord, forgive;

because many children live in fear and have not heard the good news of Jesus Christ:

O Lord, forgive;

because these great needs cannot always be met for want of skilled workers and adequate resources:

O Lord, forgive.

Let us all say this prayer together:

O Lord God, forgive what we have been;
sanctify what we are; and direct what
we shall be: for Jesus Christ's sake. Amen.

FAMILY, FRIENDS AND HOME

Home

563 Be with us, Lord, where people see us at our best and at our worst. Make our homes places where we can speak of God

without hypocrisy and serve our loved ones without self-interest; through Jesus Christ our Lord.   Amen.

564 Heavenly Father, we thank you for our homes and families, for our food and clothing and for all the happiness that parents and children can share. We ask that your love may surround us, your care protect us and that we may know your peace at all times, for Jesus's sake.   Amen.

565 Forgive us, Lord, when jealousy, greed, temper, pride or indignation disturb the peace of our family. Help us to find the right words and the right actions to soothe and heal the hurt. Forgive us when we quarrel. Help us to forgive others: help others to forgive us; through Jesus Christ our Lord.   Amen.

Marriage

566 O God our Father, who made men and women to live together in families: we pray that marriage may be held in honour; that husbands and wives may live faithfully together; and that members of every family may grow in mutual understanding, love and courtesy; through Jesus Christ our Lord.   Amen.

Parents

567 Father, grant to all parents wisdom and understanding in the upbringing of their children: that as they grow in stature so too they may learn to love you more day by day, through Jesus Christ.   Amen.

Friends

568 Today, O Lord, remember for good all our friends, for whom we thank you. Thank you for those who come to see us, or who write to us, or who are always at hand to help us. We ask you to bless them all today: some at home, some far away, some who are travelling, some who are ill, some who are sad.

Bless those, too, whom we find it hard to be friends with;
and make us true friends to one another and to the Lord Jesus
Christ, the Friend of sinners. We ask this in his
name.   Amen.

Friends and Neighbours

569 Heavenly Father, look in love on all our friends and
neighbours. Keep them from all harm; deepen our friendship
with them; and may we grow in love of you, our Saviour and
Friend, through Jesus Christ our Lord.   Amen.

Absent Friends

570 O sweet and loving Lord Christ, our unseen yet eternal
Friend, the Giver of all true friendship and the Guardian of
our love: we pray for all our friends and loved ones wherever
in your great world they may be. Bless them with the fullness
of your grace and power and fill their hearts and lives with
yourself. You alone know how much we love each other, and
the pain and loneliness of being separated. As we link our
hands in yours grant us to know the strength and peace of
your presence and the sheltering warmth and comfort of your
love; and keep us, O Lord, so near to yourself, that we may
evermore be near to each other, and, if it is your will, give us
the renewal of our fellowship on earth, and, at last, our
perfect union in the friendship of our Father's
home.   Amen.

Holidays

571 O God our Father, we thank you for the times of rest from the
normal daily round. We pray that those who are on holiday at
this time may be enabled to find the threefold recreation of
body, mind and spirit that will strengthen them for your
service in the days that lie ahead; through Jesus Christ our
Lord.   Amen.

572 Heavenly Father, because you rested from your work of
creation, we thank you for the opportunities we have of

holidays and leisure. Refresh our bodies, minds and souls, so that we may return to our daily work better able to serve you, through Jesus Christ our Lord.   Amen.

573 We thank you, our Father, that your purpose for men is that our lives should consist of work and recreation, of activity and rest, of business and holiday.

We pray for those who are now enjoying the opportunity of holidays. Enable them, we pray, to be refreshed in mind, body and spirit, so that in the coming months they may be able to work more effectively and to serve you more faithfully, through Jesus Christ our Lord.   Amen.

FAMILY PRAYERS

For the Home

574 O God, your Son Jesus Christ prepared to save the world by serving in a home: help us as a family to love and serve you and one another. Give us those blessings which will enable us to make this dwelling a worthy place for your presence, through Jesus Christ our Lord.   Amen.

For the Week

575 We give you thanks, O God our Father, for every good and perfect gift: for our work on Monday; for our games on Saturday; for our worship on Sunday; and for our Saviour Jesus Christ who is with us all through the week.   Amen.

576 We thank you, heavenly Father, for all the opportunities which will be ours during this week. We thank you for the people who will serve us in the shop and office and classroom. We thank you for those who make our life brighter, the postman and the friendly neighbour. We thank you for those who make our life easier, the dustman and the policeman. As people do so much for us, help us not to make their work a

burden but rather look for ways in which we may help others too; for Jesus Christ's sake.   Amen.

577   We thank you, Lord, that we can freely worship you. Help us, we pray, to continue our worship through the coming week by living lives which are filled with love, both for you and for all mankind.   Amen.

Morning

578   O Lord, enable us this day to reveal your glory in all we think and say and do; that your presence may bless and strengthen us all the day long, through Jesus Christ our Lord.   Amen.

579   Thank you, Father, for a quiet night. Help us in the new day that stretches before us. We do not know what it will contain; it is unknown. We only know ourselves and the problems and possibilities of our character.

Help us to be friendly and kind to one another and to others whom we shall meet. Help us to curb our impatience and the unkind words which may come to our lips.

And if we have to face danger or make decisions which are difficult, give us courage to do what we know to be right. Help us to look for opportunities of service wherever we may be and help us to remember that everything we do can be offered to you as an act of worship. So may we not be ashamed when this day is over, for Christ's sake.   Amen.

580   Fill us, O Lord, with the Holy Spirit, that we may go forth with eagerness and joy to love and serve you in holiness and to do your perfect will, through Jesus Christ our Lord.   Amen.

581   O Holy Spirit of God, Inspirer of all that is good and beautiful and true, come into our hearts this day and fill us with your light and strength. Help us to hate all sin and selfishness and to fight against them with unfaltering courage and resolve. And because we are weak and cannot prevail without your help, strengthen us and give us the victory, for Christ's sake.   Amen.

582 O God our Father, help us today to live as true men and
women. Help us to do our work as Christ did, putting duty
before pleasure, others before self, and no one before
you.   Amen.

583 O God, give us cheerfulness and courage to take up again the
duty you have appointed for each one of us. In this day of
opportunity let your Holy Spirit inspire us so that however
humble or hard our task we may do it with true faithfulness
and greatness of heart, through Jesus Christ our
Lord.   Amen.

Daily Life

584 Christ has no hands but our hands,
Christ has no feet but our feet,
Christ has no love but our love,
to tell of his goodness,
to heal the world's wounds,
to teach the way of love.

We have hands, Lord: with so many things to do, with
varying skills and a myriad tasks, but there is always time for
you.

We have feet, Lord: they take us to so many different
places on widely differing errands. Sometimes they are so
tired, Lord, and sore and weary. But they will still go for you,
Lord.

We have love, Lord: love for our husbands, wives and
children; for our friends and relations, but not always for
others, Lord—the lonely, the sick and those in pain. We have
love, Lord, for so many good things in life. Please, Lord, give
us more love for you.   Amen.

585 O God our Father, keep us your children safe under your
protection this day. May we feel the strength of your Spirit
within us, the warmth of your love around us and your
presence through all our way. Let no danger daunt us, no
temptation master us, nor any evil thing separate us from
yourself. Hear us, O Father, for your dear Son's
sake.   Amen.

For Absent Members of the Family

586 Loving Father, you are present everywhere and care for all
your children: we commend to you the member(s) of our
family now parted from us. Watch over (him), protect and
guide (him), surround (him) and us with your love and bring
us all together again in your eternal love, through Jesus
Christ our Lord.   Amen.

Thanksgiving at Night

587 Almighty God, the protector of all who trust in you, we
thank you for your goodness to us during the past day: for
work to do and health and strength to do it; for our home and
the love which binds us together with you and one another;
for protection from harm and danger, and for sins forgiven.
Receive our thanks for the sake of Jesus Christ our
Lord.   Amen.

Saturday Evening

588 Come to us, Lord Jesus, when we receive the bread of life and
the cup of salvation. Cleanse our hearts from sin that they
may be worthy of so great a guest.   Amen.

589 O God, speak to us through your word. Pour out upon us
your grace that we may learn your will and obey your call;
through Jesus Christ our Lord.   Amen.

FAMILY SERVICES AND CHILDREN'S SERVICES

The following are for different seasons and are designed to be
followed by the Alternative Service Book Confession and
Absolution.

Christmas

590 Heavenly Father, you know how much we have looked

forward to Christmas; to parties and games, to presents and crackers, to good food and fun.

We know that you like us to be happy on the birthday of Jesus, but help us to remember that it is his birthday and to thank you for sending him into the world to live like us, to show us your love and to bring us back to you. In his name we ask it. Amen.

New Year

591 As we meet together for our first family service in the New Year we thank God for all his blessings to us in the past and we pray for his help and guidance in the days ahead. We also remember the many times we have let him down and fallen short of the standard he has set us.

So we kneel to say how sorry we are, and to ask for forgiveness.

Epiphany

592 Lord, we remember how you led the Wise Men to Bethlehem by the light of a star. Guide us as we travel to the heavenly city that we and all people may know Jesus as the true and living way. Amen.

1st Sunday in Lent

593 Lent is a time when Christian men and women, boys and girls, try to think very seriously about what it means to be a follower of Jesus. We are going to do that between now and Easter at our services, in our Sunday School and in special weekly study groups.

We are going to start this morning and a good way to do that is to admit that we have not lived up to the standards which Jesus set us. So we kneel to confess and to ask for forgiveness.

Lent—Perseverance

594 Lord, we remember how Jesus persevered; through his temptations, through criticism, in the face of threats; when there was little response to his work, when his own disciples were disloyal at his trial.

Help us to keep on trying and not to give up when things seem difficult. We ask this through Jesus Christ our Lord.   Amen.

Mothering Sunday

595 Today is Mothering Sunday. We have all come to church to praise God: to thank him for the loving devotion of our parents, particularly our mothers; to thank him for all they do for us and for all they mean to us; to thank him for the happiness of our family life, and for our homes.

We thank him for our spiritual mother, the church, whose family we joined at our baptism and through whom we are taught the faith of Christ crucified and have our footsteps guided in the way of peace.

But first we admit our unworthiness and ask God's forgiveness for the things we have done wrong.

Mothering Sunday

596 The theme of our service today is gratitude for our homes and for the love and care of our parents. Too many people just take it all for granted and never think of saying 'Thank you'.

Mothering Sunday gives us the chance to think about it and to tell God that we are sorry for our forgetfulness.

Palm Sunday

597 On this Palm Sunday, we thank you, heavenly Father, for the children and grown-ups who cheered as Jesus entered Jerusalem long ago, and who laid palms and coats in his path.

Help us like them to enjoy singing hymns of worship and praise and to use our voices to glorify you. But first we remember our unworthiness and ask your forgiveness for the things we have done wrong.

Pentecost

598 Today is Whit Sunday. We also call it Pentecost, because the Spirit of God came and filled the hearts of Jesus's disciples on the day of Pentecost. That is what we remember today.

The Spirit of God is the wonderful Spirit who lived in Jesus. We call this Spirit the Holy Spirit.

Today we remember that Jesus wants this Spirit to live in us too, so that we may really be his brothers and sisters, and really live as sons and daughters of God.

And we begin by telling God about the things we have done wrong and are sorry about.

Trinity Sunday

599 Trinity Sunday is a time to think especially about our worship of God.

We worship him because he is Lord of the world, the stars and space. We praise him because he made everything so wonderfully. We thank him because we know that every good thing comes from him. We know that he is all goodness, that he is a holy God. So first we shall say we are sorry for the times we have failed, and then we can come to worship him in the beauty of holiness.

Christian Aid Week

600 At the beginning of Christian Aid week we remember the words of Jesus that those who give food to the hungry, drink to the thirsty, take in the stranger, clothe the naked, help the sick, and visit the prisoner, do it for him.

We are ashamed that we so often forget this; that we often grumble about our own situation when we have so much.

Let us kneel down and confess our failings and our lack of real concern.

Christian Aid Week

601 We have come together at the start of Christian Aid week to recall the great message of love that our Lord Jesus Christ taught us, and to see how it can be expressed, in our world and in our time.

But first let us acknowledge that our greed and selfishness are part of the cause of the divisions between rich and poor in the world, for we have broken his command to love.

Any Sunday

602 God our Father, be with us in our time of worship. When we pray, help us to concentrate our thoughts on you; when we listen to the reading of the Bible, help us to understand it; when we sing your praise help us to sing because we really love you: help us to worship you in spirit and in truth, through Jesus Christ our Lord.   Amen.

A Children's Litany

603 For calling us into your great family of love; for making us your sons and daughters; for putting your Spirit into our hearts; for helping us to grow up into Christ:
  O God, we thank and praise you.
For signing us with the sign of the cross; for calling us to be your faithful soldiers and servants; for giving us a cause to fight for; for equipping us for your holy warfare:
  O God, we thank and praise you.
For knowing our abilities and powers; for calling us to work together; for giving us strength through fellowship; for making us united in your service:
  O God, we thank and praise you.
Help us to know you more and more; help us to know the Bible and to love it; teach us how to talk to you and how to listen to you; teach us to pray.
  In your mercy: hear our prayer.
Help us to see the needs of other people; help us to want to help; teach us how to do good; make us more and more

practical day by day.

In your mercy: hear our prayer.

Help us to see and know your will for our lives; show us what you want us to become; lead us into jobs and hobbies and friendships which will please you and fulfill our being.

In your mercy: hear our prayer.

Bless our church, our Sunday School, its day school, its scouts and guides and cub scouts and brownies and its youth clubs.

O Lord, bless us all.

Bless all the babies who are baptized in this church and bless their mothers and fathers and godparents. Help us to help the babies to grow up as true Christians, full members of the church, and true servants of mankind.

O Lord, bless us all.

Comfort those who are sick or sad, make them brave in their suffering and bring them safely out of all their trouble.

In your mercy: hear our prayer.

Bless all the peoples of the world and bring them to know and love you through Jesus Christ our Lord and grant that from this knowledge they may arrange their lives and organize the world in righteousness and peace.

In your mercy: hear our prayer.

A Confession

604 O Lord Jesus Christ, we confess to you now the wrong things we have done, the wrong words we have said, the wrong in our hearts. Please forgive us and help us to live as you want us to. Amen.

A Thanksgiving

605 We thank you, God, for our homes: our mothers and fathers, our brothers and sisters and the others in our family; for all our friends in the same road. Help us to love and be friends with all of them, to have no fighting, no quarrels, no bitter thoughts; but to behave in such a way that everyone else may be glad to have us living near them, in the name of Jesus Christ, whom boys and girls were always glad to meet. Amen.

A Trusting Prayer

606 Lord Jesus, we ask you to help us to remember that you are
our Friend and Saviour, wherever we are and whatever we do:
be with us in our work and in our games, our home and our
school, our church and our Sunday School and help us to love
you and trust you every day of our lives.   Amen.

For Other Children Who Are Ill

607 Lord Jesus Christ, please be very near to those who are sick
and in hospital, especially..., and anyone else we know.
Help them to get better soon; help their families not to worry
about them; and help the doctors and nurses to do their work
well.   Amen.

For a Mission Hospital

608 Thank you, Lord God, for your hospital and missions at...
and for your servants who look after it; thank you too for those
who have told us about the things they need in order to do
their work there; thank you for helping us to give our money
to help meet that need and accept our gifts as we bring them
to you now. May they help to bring healing and strength of
body, mind and spirit to many people, through Jesus Christ
our Lord.   Amen.

A Thanksgiving for Jesus

609 Thank you, Lord Jesus, for stopping to listen to every sick
person who called out to you; thank you for healing every
kind of sickness there is, for feeding the hungry, for setting
men free and for raising the dead. Bless all the people all over
the world who are trying to follow your example. Bless those
who are taking food to the hungry people, medicine to sick
people, proper forms of government to nations which do not
have real freedom and your holy gospel to those whose love for
other people is dead. Bless them all, and all the sick, sad and
lonely people to whom they go, for your dear name's
sake.   Amen.

An Act of Thanksgiving and Intercession

610 For all your gifts, O Lord,
> *we thank you.*

For health and strength and life itself,
> *we thank you.*

For our friends, our homes, our families,
> *we thank you.*

For our church and our worship,
> *we thank you.*

For every chance to serve you,
> *we thank you.*

For Jesus Christ our Lord,
> *we thank you.*

And now we pray for all who govern our land,
> *we ask you to bless them.*

For all who minister in our church,
> *we ask you to bless them.*

For all who provide for our daily needs,
> *we ask you to bless them.*

For all who do not yet know you,
> *we ask you to bless them.*

For all who are tired, or ill, or lonely,
> *we ask you to bless them.*

Hear these prayers, O Lord our God, for Jesus' sake.   Amen.

At All Saints Tide

611 For all the men and women, boys and girls, who love and
serve you,
> *we thank you, God.*

For everybody who makes Jesus real to other people,
> *we thank you, God.*

For everyone who has taught about you by the way they
think, the way they act, and by what they say,
> *we thank you, God.*

For everyone who helps those who are sick or sad, and for all those who are brave and patient when things are going wrong,

> *we thank you, God.*

Dear God, may we know you better and better, so that we may love you more and more and serve you with all our hearts,

> *please, God, hear us.*

May we help those in need; may they know that God is real and that God is love,

> *please, God, hear us.*

May we be friends with you, friends with all your children, friends with one another,

> *please, God, hear us.*

PRAYERS OF PERSONAL DEVOTION

'God Be In My Heart and In My Thinking'

612 God be in my heart—

> Heavenly Father, we were taught by your Son Jesus Christ that the pure in heart shall see God. Cleanse our hearts from all impurity; give us such hatred of all that is evil, and such love for all that is strong and beautiful, that we may be delivered from temptation and become a strength to others who are tempted.

—and in my thinking.

> God of truth, you have guided people in the quest for knowledge down the centuries. Help us in our study to use your gifts of wisdom and understanding, that by them we may humbly embrace all wise teaching and be led into all truth.

God be in my heart—

> By your grace may our hearts be filled with good thoughts and our lives be filled with generous actions; by your grace may our hearts never forget our Saviour or think that any other life is worthier to be followed than his; by your grace, may our hearts love others, as our Saviour's did, and may we so live that all may give glory to him for ever.

—and in my thinking.

> Father, enlarge the range of our thinking, of our
> loyalty, of our devotion. By thinking deeply for one
> cause may we not limit our sensitiveness to other
> needs and claims. Deliver us from prejudice and
> narrowness in our thinking, from party loyalties that
> separate rather than unite us. Direct our thoughts to
> the wonder and richness of the worldwide church
> which lives through the variety of gifts that are
> brought by all.

God be in my heart—

> Lord, you are worthier of a greater love than our poor
> hearts can either give or understand. Fill our hearts
> with such love that we may grow daily more like our
> Saviour and finally achieve the crown of love which he
> promised to those hearts which love him.

—and in my thinking.

> Loving Father, may we know that which is worth
> knowing; distinguish between the fleeting and the
> eternal, between the visible and the spiritual, so that
> the light of your truth may shine in our hearts.

A Morning Prayer

613 Lord, Leader, Director, Friend: as this new day begins,
whether grey or bright, inside the necessary boundaries of
family, work, place and time: thank you for the great gift of
freedom contained within this day's activities. Help me to
use it carefully and the freedoms of others gently,
remembering the importance of choice. So help us especially
to follow you.   Amen.

At the 'Eleventh Hour'

614 Father in heaven, help us to accept and understand that we
who labour in your name our whole life long receive no more
reward than those who find you only as the daylight
dies.   Amen.

For Abundant Life

615 Father, give us not what we have earned, but your abundant life. And not to ourselves alone but to all your children, whenever they should find you.   Amen.

For Love

616 Father, help us to realize that we must not love people because we need them, rather we must need them because we love them.   Amen.

617 Father, rich and poor are only rich and poor in your love. No one is rich without your love. No one is poor who has your love. Father, Jesus died to give us a life of love. Help us to learn from Jesus.   Amen.

For Patience

618 Heavenly Father, we confess that so much frustration and conflict comes from our impetuosity and impatience. Help us to live at your pace. Slow us down. May our lives achieve the rhythm of your pulse, beating with strength and security and steadiness, and the spiritual health and wholeness which you desire for your children. Help us to be so conscious of your presence with us now that we abandon the hurry towards the future. Teach us the many benefits of contentment. Encourage our faith; through Jesus Christ our Lord.   Amen.

For Faith

619   Lord I believe, help with my unbelief,
            For I believe in your deep love and mercy,
            In your forgiving understanding
            Of the human heart.
            Through the lonely watches of the spirit's night
            Within the narrow tunnel of my grief,
            I know a quiet dawn will come.
            Tortured alone in the creeping, loathsome dark
            And dragged along a labyrinthine maze,

I still believe your healing sun
Will bring the birth of some new day
To break the iron gates of pain,
To bring, again, life where hopes, broken, lie
Crippled among her ancient battlements;
Lord, I believe that there will surely be
Light, after the midnight burns to death.

On Being Known

620   Lord, you have known my downsitting
And my uprising—the come and go
Of life's long littleness,
The moments of departure and arrival,
Waking and lapsing into unconsciousness,
Setting out for the market place
Or back from the fields;
To the longest working day
You saw me go.

You noticed me and knew about
The unimportant times (as I thought of them).
You loved me all the way
As I returned from the far country,
From the land of no-pasture
Back to an inheritance;
Through unseen watchfulness,
When human love forgot,
You welcomed me.

To Use the Mind

621 Father of heaven and earth, you are the source of all
knowledge and of all wisdom. All that we are and all that we
have stems from your power and your presence. You have
given us our minds and the ability to understand and
appreciate all that is good and true and lovely. But you leave
us with a choice: the choice of doing your will or following
our own inclinations.

As you have given us the power to understand, give us also
the strength to accept and to follow your life and example,
that our learning may be for your glory and the well-being of
all your people; through Jesus Christ our Lord.   Amen.

People and Places

622 I feel you near, Lord, when I am in stillness.
But I know your presence most when I mix with other people:
when I share with them the experience of living,
the joys of the gospel, the agonies of life.

Lord you come to me through people and places:
through great cathedrals and wide open spaces.
May you come to others, Lord, through me.
May others find your love, in what I say and do and
am.   Amen.

For Openness

623 God our Father, we lack so many gifts and we fail so often.
We lack the humility to listen and learn; our arrogance closes
our hands and hearts to the gifts we need from you and from
others. Our pride condemns us to choose the path that leads
to loneliness, that breeds despair.

Break down our isolation, remove the barriers that separate
us from the world and our fellow men. Help us, Lord, to
receive as well as give, to learn as well as to teach, to accept
love as well as to give love.

Help us to recognize our need of others; but above all open
our hearts to the need of yourself.   Amen.

Peter, John and James

624 Lord, like Peter, John and James, we are human. And our
humanity is a precious gift from you. Help us not to make it
an excuse for weakness and wrong-doing, but a foundation on

which to build that perfect humanity displayed in your Son, Jesus Christ.   Amen.

The Love of Christ

625 Lord Jesus Christ, your love for your disciples never wavered. By love you led them from misunderstanding to acceptance; by love you turned their doubt into faith; by love you brought them closer to you.

   That same love is ours also. Help us to understand and to accept it; so that our lives may be transformed and renewed.   Amen.

ARROW PRAYERS

626 If, Lord, we choose to wash other people's feet, let there be no vanity in us.   Amen.

627 To those with a quiet tongue and simple manners, Lord, impress upon them the value of their silent witness, we pray.   Amen.

628 Forgive us, Lord, for being afraid and give us your strength.   Amen.

629 We pray that in our words to each other we may be simple, sparing, loving, wise. May we live in the way of Christ, using words in his way.   Amen.

630 Sweep away the darkness of apprehension and sweeten our ways with the sanity of wholesome laughter.   Amen.

631 Christ Jesus, simple man and son of mother Mary, we do not come to you in search of earthly power, but to ask for a quiet mind, so that we, too, may work with your simplicity.   Amen.

632 Help us to tell others, Lord, of what you are. Help us to do it sensibly, tolerantly, happily, easily, strongly and with your beauty.   Amen.

633 Help us, Lord, to make our words sparkle with your joy.   Amen.

634 Sometimes you enable your servants to speak about you so clearly that even the nations of the earth will listen. Bless those who do this in your name. Help us to listen.   Amen.

635 Beset as we are with damaged bodies, troubled souls and tired minds, Lord, may we turn to you as children to their Father, for comfort and strength.   Amen.

636 If we identify evil in us or around, let us be swift to call on your name, O God.   Amen.

637 When earning a living takes all our strength, O Lord, help us to cultivate times of quiet and tune our minds to yours. So give us power and so make us calm.

Blessings

638 May Christ, who is so powerfully normal, be with you every minute of each night and day.   Amen.

639 May you leave this place in the serenity of God.   Amen.

640 Go your separate ways still joined by the love of Christ.   Amen.

641 Now you are bound by the love of God you will not be scattered by the winds of the devil. Be strong in mind, be together in purpose, be uplifted in thought; by the controlling power of Christ.   Amen.

642 In Christ's name we surround ourselves with his powerful protection, safe from harm, totally depending upon the supreme light of his presence.   Amen.

643 May the total power of God enter you, make you spiritually awake, eager for action, abundantly strong, perceptive, and wise, to act as a Christian.   Amen.

644 **For Community**

Eternal Creator of the universe: you created man and woman and we are proud of our direct link with you. We pray for grace to walk with you and speak with you, that the bond you made between us may develop according to your word.   Amen.

645 Draw together, Lord Christ, the group of people we live among. With you at the head of the group, Lord, help us to join ourselves together with humour, contentment, mutual support and warm generosity.   Amen.

646 Almighty God, we can see your design in all good things around us. Stimulate our minds and hearts to identify and acknowledge our bond with all you have made and to live in harmony according to your design.   Amen.

PRAYERS FOR HEALING

Laying on of Hands: Mark 1:29–34

647 Heavenly Father, your Son Jesus Christ brought health and healing to those who came to him. May we be touched anew by him, that we may feel your love, may obey his will and be raised up by the Holy Spirit, strengthened for your service.   Amen.

Blindness: Mark 10:46–52

648 Creator God, through whose Son Jesus Christ lost sight is restored: have mercy on the physically or spiritually blind, meet them in their need, that enlightened by your Spirit they may follow in the way of Jesus.   Amen.

Cleansing: Mark 1:40–44

649 Holy God and loving Father, we come to you in prayer, stained by sin, tarnished by evil, often rejected and despising ourselves: in your compassion, touch, cleanse and restore us, that others may see in us your new creation and we rejoice in the liberty of being your children; in and through Jesus Christ our Saviour.   Amen.

Deliverance: Mark 4:35 – 5:20

650 Lord God, whose Son Jesus Christ stills the storms around us and within, free us from all that has us in its grip, speak your word of peace and restoration to our disorders in nation, church and home, that a right mind may be ours again; in the name of Jesus we ask it.   Amen.

Fear: John 20:19–23

651 Lord Jesus Christ, come through the locked doors of our lives and stand in our area of fear. Speak your word of peace; show us your wounds in which are our healing; breathe anew your Holy Spirit upon us, that, filled with his perfect love and freed from fear, we may obey your sending and go with new power and authority to heal your world.   Amen.

Paralysis: Luke 5:17–26

652 Lord God, whose power was present to heal those who came to Jesus and to raise up those paralysed by sin, give us a truer awareness of our needs—to the paralysis of our guilt, come with forgiveness; to wills weakened by indecision, come with truth; to lives restricted by fear and doubts, come with your Spirit's love and power.   Amen.

Forgiveness: Matthew 18:21–35; Ephesians 4:32

653 Heavenly Father, whose forgiveness of us rests on our forgiveness of others; send your Spirit to change our hearts

and heal our memories, that we may be free to forgive; even as
you, in Christ, forgive us.   Amen.

Relationships: Mark 14:3–9

654 Heavenly Father, you rejoice in your children's acts of love;
free us from fear and insecurity that criticizes and condemns,
and give us the love of Christ in our hearts, that we may
rejoice and be enriched by the differences of others, who are
your gift to us.   Amen.

655 Lord Jesus Christ: that I may love you totally and my
neighbour as myself, touch and heal my relationship with
you; touch and heal my relationship with myself; touch and
heal my relationship with others; that healed, I may heal;
that reconciled, I may reconcile; that renewed, I may renew;
that raised up, I may raise others, not in my power or
strength, but in and through your name, Jesus Saviour of the
world.   Amen.

Freed to Heal

656 Lord Jesus Christ, who healed those who came to you and
then commanded them to go forth in your name. Touch this
day not only our lives but our ears, that we may hear and obey
your command to go, freed from a sick preoccupation with
healing, but healthily preoccupied to heal your
world.   Amen.

For a Sick Person: a Prayer and a Blessing

657 Heavenly Father, your Son Jesus Christ ministered to those
who were ill. Touch . . . now, that (he) may know your
presence, feel your love and receive your strength.

May the Father's love enfold you; the presence of Christ
remain with you; the healing Spirit work within you: that
you may be raised up into new health, new wholeness and
new holiness.   Amen.

The Future: Matthew 6:5–13, 25–34

658 Heavenly Father, who has taught us by your Son not to be over-anxious about tomorrow, because you care for us and know our needs: relieve us of the burden of the future and enable us to trust you as your children. Help us not to cling to life but to lose it; for the sake of him whose yoke is easy and whose burden light, Jesus Christ our Lord.   Amen.

Index of Writers

Ablewhite, Stanley   456–458
Arnold, Roy   613
Autton, Norman   400–406, 409,
    415–420, 428, 429

Bailey, Gordon   200, 201, 618
Barker, Walter   363, 364
Bates, Bishop Gordon   130–132,
    621–625
Baynes, Simon   30, 61, 95,
    281, 303, 327, 342, 390, 432,
    440, 441
Berryman, Richard   408
Best, Frank   487
Blakey, Elsie   503
Botting, Michael (from the collection
    edited by M. H. Botting)   28, 34,
    57, 76–78, 142, 154, 183, 192,
    253, 282, 305, 389, 427, 433,
    442, 564, 566, 569, 572
Bunting, Ian   43, 54, 56, 157–164,
    167, 288, 434, 563, 576

Casson, Stanley   29

Dudley-Smith, Bishop Timothy
    324, 329, 348, 349, 544

Evans, Harold E.   98, 300,
    316, 570, 580–583, 585

Farrell, John   426, 614–617
Farrell, Tom   315
Francis, Joyce   99, 143, 155, 333,
    367, 567

Girdlestone, Margaret   534
Godson, Alan   156, 196
Goodacre, Kathleen   545–547, 549
Greet, Dr. Kenneth   289–291

Hampson, Marjorie   398, 528, 529
Hampson, William   294–296, 448,
    449, 529
Hay, Marjorie   393
Heywood, Susan   195, 392
Houghton, Elizabeth   471
Hume, Cardinal Basil   293

Idle, Christopher   27, 58, 59, 122,
    124–127, 191, 203, 259,
    277–280, 297, 313, 321, 322,
    356–358, 365, 373, 395, 421,
    438, 439, 443, 452, 454, 460,
    465, 469, 486, 493, 507,
    515–517, 537, 538, 548, 550,
    568, 575, 577, 604–607, 610

Jenkins, Eric   490–491

Lambert-Smith, Henry   335, 336
Liverpool Cathedral   42, 275, 345,
    347, 478, 562
Lloyd, Meirion   41

Manwaring, Randle   510, 619, 620
Markby, Peter   260, 332, 343, 450,
    453, 463, 540, 573
McIntyre, Very Rev. Prof.
    John   292
Mitchell, Patricia   33, 39, 40, 64,

165, 166, 168, 286, 328, 346,
366, 376–383, 385, 391, 399,
410–412, 430, 505, 525, 526,
565

Morris, John   65, 584

Nash-Williams, Piers   60
Neale, Eddie   473, 475
Netherwood, Anne   302
Nugent, Alan   368–370

Owens, F. O.   264

Pegler, Douglas   265
Poole, J. W.   274
Pope John Paul   341
Price, John Wheatley   184, 359,
360
Pritchard, Peter   425, 508, 509,
551–554, 558–561, 590–597,
599–602, 612

Reynolds, P. D.   533
Richards, John   197, 647–658
Rybot, Doris   266

Saward, Michael   311, 317, 372,
374, 578
Searle, John   62, 67, 68, 123, 128,
129, 145, 146, 169, 170, 202,
207, 261, 334
Smith, Lucy   387
Street, F. W.   574, 586–589

Thornton, Audrey   555–557
Thornton, Kenneth   518–522, 527
Thorp, R. C.   141

Warner, Andrew   50, 66, 257, 263,
396, 422, 445, 466–468, 514,
530, 539, 543
Watson, L.   276
Wilcox, Donald   626–646
Williams, Alison   523, 524
Williams, Dick   1–5, 8, 10, 12, 15,
18, 21–24, 35–38, 44, 45, 48,
49, 51, 55, 63, 69, 70, 71, 96,
97, 100, 101, 133–140, 144,
147, 150–153, 182, 187–190,
198, 199, 204, 251, 252, 254–
256, 267–273, 283–285, 287,
299, 304, 307, 308, 312, 314,
319, 325, 326, 330, 331, 337–
340, 350–355, 361, 362, 371,
375, 384, 386, 388, 394, 397,
407, 423, 424, 431, 435, 436,
446, 455, 459, 461, 462, 464,
470, 474, 476, 477, 479–485,
488, 489, 494–496, 506,
511–513, 535, 536, 541, 542,
598, 603, 608, 609, 611
Williams, Susan   6, 7, 9, 11, 13,
14, 16, 17, 19, 20, 25, 26, 31,
32, 46, 47, 52, 53, 72–75, 79–
94, 102–121, 148–149, 171–
181, 185, 186, 193, 194, 205,
206, 208–250, 298, 444, 447,
472, 531, 532
Wood, Bishop Maurice   301, 309,
310, 318
Woolf, Bernard   437, 571
Worsdall, J. R.   258, 262, 282

Index of Topics

Advent 23–56
Aged 144, 343, 395, 396
Agricultural Research 255
Agricultural Workers 254, 259
Air Travel 486, 489
All Saints 294–296, 611
Alone, Those Living 455
Animals 262–266
Anniversary, Church 337, 339
Architects 338
'Arrow' Prayers 626–637
Art and Artists 42, 312, 346, 496–504
Ascension 182–186
Ash Wednesday 95–101
Astronauts 492–495

Bible 30–42, 191, 365, 602, 603
Bishops 48, 49
Boredom 476
Broadcasting 513
Broken Homes 430, 530–532
Building a Church 336–338

Children 377–381, 408, 525, 533–540, 543
Children's Prayers 67–71, 139–140, 145, 202, 207, 261, 523, 524, 603–611
Christian Aid Week 600, 601
see also One World Week
Christmas 57–76
Church, the 317–339
Church Councils 331–334
City, the 72, 76, 130, 302, 471, 485, 592
Civil Strife 314
Clergy 49, 50, 321, 329, 411
Closed Lands, the Church in 365, 366
Colleges 51, 541–561
Committee Meetings 331–334
Communication 492, 513, 622
Creation 1–7
Crime and Criminals 137, 444, 477
Cross of Christ, the 10, 56, 102, 106, 111–113, 119, 131, 143, 155, 314
Depression 157, 224, 398, 619
Deprived Children 473–475
Destitute, the 471
Disabled, the 407–408
Disasters 425, 431
Divorced, the 530–532
Doctors 389, 411, 453
Doubt 158, 166, 181, 211, 619, 625
Drug Addicts 466, 468

Easter 147–170
Ecumenism 341–347
see also One World Week
Education 541, 558
Employers and Employed 448–451
Epiphany 76–80
Evangelism 192–197
Examinations 559

Family Breakdown 473, 530, 532
Family Life 346, 359, 454, 526,

533, 564, 586
Family Prayers   574–589
Family Services, Introductions
   to 590–603
Farmers   254, 256, 258, 259, 456–458
Fasting   101
Food   258–262, 564, 590
Friends   125, 151, 302, 522, 568–570

Generation Gap   533, 534
Godparents   386, 537, 603 (para 8)
Good Friday   132, 144–146
Government(s)   15, 21, 134, 233, 234, 255, 268, 285, 306, 308, 436, 445, 454, 459, 609
Guidance   60, 76, 81, 96, 331–334, 511

Handicapped   68, 278, 292, 392, 407, 408 ·
Harvest   251–261
Healing   20, 71, 409–416, 647–651
Heaven   249, 250, 507
Holidays   373, 453, 571–573
Holy Spirit   189–203, 220–221, 382–385, 580–583
Holy Week   130–146
Homeless, the   61, 71, 124, 328, 432, 438
Homes   57, 154, 563, 564
Hope   23–29, 54, 245, 246
Hospitals   390, 401, 405, 411, 415, 416

Immigrants   445, 446
Industry   73, 272, 448–452

Jews, the   361–364
Journalists   42, 287, 512
Judges   135, 478, 480

Law   214, 231, 306, 445, 478, 480–482

Lent   95–146
Lifestyle   3, 72, 77, 79, 81, 87, 206, 208, 273, 618

Marriage   515–529, 566
Mass Media   513
Maundy Thursday   131
Mental Illness   397–398
Mission(s)   70, 78, 103, 185, 215, 328, 651
Missionaries   354, 355, 357, 359, 360, 370
Money   85, 219, 276, 442, 443, 462
Mothers   59, 122, 123, 128, 595, 596
Music   346, 505–510

Nation(s)   267–273, 303–316
New Year   297–302, 591
Novelists   511–512
Nurses   387, 389, 411, 453, 521

One World Week   267–273
Ordination Retreat   348–349

Palm Sunday   130
Parish Missions   371
Parliament   305, 313
Parochial Church Councils   331–334
Peace   91, 113, 190, 274–293
Pentecost   189–203, 598
Persecution   21, 144, 320
Police   483, 484, 576
Preachers   189, 203, 350
Prisoners   144, 187, 346, 477–478, 600
Prison Officers   478, 479
Psychiatrists   423

Queen, the   303–308, 313

Racial Divisions   73, 274, 282, 288, 445, 446
Redundancy   454, 458, 459, 461

Refugees 61, 440
Religions, Other 367–368
Remembrance Sunday 274–293
Renewal 217, 237, 297, 324, 347
Research 422, 490–495
Resurrection 147–176
Retreats 348, 349
Road Safety 486–488
Royal Family 305, 313

Saints 294–296, 611
Schools 541–561
Science and Scientists 5, 20, 272, 411, 490–495
Sick, the 387–408, 536, 414, 603, 610
Sick Visitors 415–418
Soldiers 286
Space Travel and Research 207, 492–495
Sport 464, 465
Stewardship 273
Sunday Schools 376–381

Teachers 545, 560, 561
Theologians 38, 330
Theological Colleges 51
Thinkers 511–514
Trades Unions 449, 450
Translators 33, 37, 41, 42
Travellers 486–489

Underprivileged, the 432–440
Unemployed, the 124, 133, 454, 459, 461
United Nations 275
    see also One World Week
Unity 341–347

Vandalism 444, 472

War see Remembrance Sunday
Work 127, 154, 452, 453
Worry 84, 100, 170
Writers 42, 511–514

Young People 373, 382, 383, 539, 562, 603